MILITARY ATTACHÉ IN MOSCOW

MAJOR-GENERAL
RICHARD HILTON

MILITARY ATTACHÉ in MOSCOW

Boston : THE BEACON PRESS
London: HOLLIS & CARTER

First published in Great Britain
1949
Published in the United States
1951

PRINTED AND MADE IN GREAT BRITAIN
FOR HOLLIS & CARTER LTD, LONDON
AND THE BEACON PRESS, BOSTON

CONTENTS

v

EXPLANATORY NOTES ON SOVIET ABBREVIATIONS

EXTENSIVE use of abbreviations is fashionable in the Soviet Union, particularly to denote various governmental organizations. Some of these abbreviations have been used for convenience in this book.

1. M.V.D.

These initials stand for *Ministerstvo Vnutrenniikh D'el* (The Ministry of Internal Affairs)—i.e. the Ministry of the Interior or, as we should say, the Home Office. The full name is often shortened to *Min-vnu-d'el*. This department used till recently to be called the *Narodnii Komissariat Vnutrenniikh D'el* or the *Narkomvnud'el*, from which came the initials N.K.V.D. by which the notorious political police force of the U.S.S.R. is more widely known to the world.

The M.V.D. is the old N.K.V.D. under a new name. In this book it will be called by its present name of M.V.D. Though these initials, strictly speaking, stand for the Ministry of the Interior as a whole, they have come to be attached in popular imagination throughout the U.S.S.R. to that governmental department's terrible and sinister police force. This instrument of oppression has existed since pre-revolutionary days under the following successive names: (*a*) *Okhrana* (in Tsarist times), (*b*) The Red Guard (early revolutionary days), (*c*) The CH.K. or Cheka (short for *Chrezviichainaya Komissia*, or Extraordinary Commission. Under this name it achieved its early notoriety of terror, and to this day it is still so called by many of the country people), (*d*) The G.P.U., or

vii

O.G.P.U., standing respectively for *Gosudarstvennoe Politicheskoe Upravlenie* or for *Ob'edinennoe Gosudarstvennoe Politicheskoe Upravlenie* (State Political Department or Central State Political Department), (*e*) N.K.V.D. (already explained), and finally (*f*) M.V.D. (already explained). It is a part of the technique of police terrorism to disguise this sinister force under some outwardly innocuous name, and to change the name from time to time, apparently when the name begins to stink too much, even in the nostrils of the authorities. This note may help some readers who may possibly have been puzzled by the apparent multiplicity of secret police forces under various names. 'A rose by any other name will smell as sweet.' The instrument of police tyranny, described in this book under the name M.V.D., is the Cheka or the O.G.P.U. or the N.K.V.D. There is, and has always been, only one such force. It is quite enough.

2. Intourist. Abbreviation for the Department for handling Foreign Tourist Traffic. Its activities are explained in this book.

3. VOKS. Abbreviation for the Society for Cultural Relations with Foreign Countries. This organization, posing as an amicable society rather than a government department, used to organize the visits of distinguished foreigners, predominantly those of leftist political persuasion, as guests of 'Russia' for a short personally-conducted sojourn. It has possibly fallen into disuse recently.

4. Polit-Buro. The Central Committee of the Communist Party of the U.S.S.R. About fourteen men. The real rulers of Russia.

CHAPTER I

SCOPE AND OBJECT OF THIS BOOK

SINCE my return from Moscow a few months ago I have been asked to give lectures to various types of audiences on the U.S.S.R. and connected subjects. Invariably during the period set aside for questions at the end of each lecture I have been bombarded with so many and such varied questions that it has become obvious to me that the general public does still want to know more about Russia.

This book is an attempt to answer some of the questions that have been most frequently asked, as far as they can be answered by one man after two years' work as a foreigner among the Russians. During my year in Moscow and my previous year with a British mission at Marshal Sokolovsky's Headquarters in Potsdam I kept a diary in my own personal code, wherein I recorded fully my daily journeys and experiences, my impressions of the moment, based on what I saw, heard, and personally experienced. This diary, used as an *aide-memoire* and book of reference, has provided the material for this present venture.

Most recent books on Russia have been from the pens either of Soviet citizens who have seen the light of Western civilization at a certain stage in their Communist careers, or else of foreign visitors to Russia who have gone to that country as guests of Soviet officialdom. These two points of view are very valuable indeed for giving the ordinary reader a peep behind the 'Iron Curtain', but they still leave the reader rather bewildered and perplexed. The one point of view tends to blacken everything in the Communist world which the writer has left behind him. The other tends to view the Soviet world through rose-tinted glasses, and to give an impression that 'everything in the garden is lovely'. One of the questions most frequently asked after my lectures has been concerning Victor Kravchenko's book, *I Chose Freedom*. I am usually asked whether I believe it to be grossly exaggerated or really true to life. People who have not seen Communism holding the reins of power seem to find it hard to believe that such things as he describes in that book can really happen in our modern world.

I am neither a converted Soviet citizen nor a foreigner of Left-Wing sympathies writing about the wonders that he may have seen in a brief personally-conducted tour. I am merely a soldier, who spent two years of his service among our late allies, and who had opportunities of studying the reality behind the impressive façade which is presented to the invited globe-trotter.

I do not claim to be unbiased, for surely no man of ripe age can be completely unbiased unless he is an imbecile. It so happens that my father was a staunch Liberal of very progressive views, so I cannot be accused of having grown up in a reactionary or 'die-hard Tory' atmosphere. Like most professional British soldiers, I have been inclined to leave politics to the politicians, but such political views as I may have held most of my life have undoubtedly been slightly to the Right.

When I first heard, in 1947, that I was about to get

2

a liaison job with the Russians, I was thrilled and delighted. I determined to see everything with as open and unbiased a mind as possible. As a soldier I felt genuine admiration for the recent achievements of the Red Army in hurling the *Wehrmacht* back from the Volga to the Elbe. As a staff officer I knew that the mere advance of several million Soviet soldiers over such a distance must have imposed considerable problems of organization, transport, and supply. A nation and government who could achieve such feats as this could not, in my opinion, be as bad as some detractors made them out to be. Thus I approached my new contacts with about as fairly balanced preconceptions as any grown man can expect to hold. Any adverse prejudices that I may have held as a Conservative of mild hue were more than counterbalanced by the professional admiration of a soldier for good soldiers.

When my time came to go to Moscow as military attaché, kind friends advised me to read this book or that on Russia before I went. This I stubbornly declined to do, because I still wanted to see Russia with my own unaided eyes, and not through the pages of Kravchenko on the one hand or the Dean of Canterbury on the other. Even after six months in Moscow, when I began to read some of these books, to compare them with my own personal impressions, I still made it a rule to read alternately first from one side of the ideological fence and then from the other. Left Wing literature, which I studied while in Moscow, included the following: *Socialism Victorious* by Stalin, Molotov, and others; the published speeches of

3

Lenin and Stalin; various lives of Lenin and Stalin; the official school history of the revolution and its after years; various essays by Stalin; a large part of *Das Kapital* by Marx. Also several English books by admirers of Sovietism—e.g. Miss Violet Lansbury, the Dean of Canterbury, and others. During my first few months in Russia I also studied regularly the Soviet point of view as propounded in *Pravda*, *Izvestia*, and the *New Times*. So, though I would be the last person to claim that this book is unbiased, it is at least about as unbiased as it is possible to make it.

Practically everything stated in this book will be based on what I myself saw, heard, or experienced, and not upon hearsay evidence. When it becomes necessary to resort to the latter, the fact that it is only hearsay will be clearly stated. In the welter of propaganda which exists all over the world it is possible to prove almost any point of view by quoting the right sources. My object will be to present the truth as I saw it, not to try to convert anyone to my own point of view. My personal opinions will be freely expressed, for a book on such a subject would be a gutless and colourless affair without them. It is a matter of indifference to me whether readers agree with my conclusions or not. The truth exists, and in the long run it will prevail.

CHAPTER II

THE STRANGER WITHIN THEIR GATES

MANY people imagine that one has to live for only a few months behind the 'Iron Curtain' to know the answers to most of the questions which are perplexing decent, reasonable-minded men and women all over the non-Soviet world today. What do the ordinary Russian people think about this or that? What is really worrying Stalin and the Soviet government? What is the reaction of the more intelligent Russians to the failure to settle differences amicably between East and West? These and many similar questions have been asked of me by people who have travelled extensively themselves, and who naturally judge the Soviet Union by the normal standards of civilized countries. It would indeed be ridiculous that a man with any interest in his neighbours should live for a year in France, for example, or the U.S.A. without acquiring a comprehensive knowledge of public opinion in general, and probably some idea of the attitude of leading public men toward current affairs.

The U.S.S.R. cannot be judged by the normal standards of civilized countries—above all in its attitude toward foreigners resident within its borders. This peculiar attitude exercises such a strong influence upon the foreign observer that it cannot fail to colour everything that the foreign observer sees and registers in his mind. Without some understanding of this attitude it would be impossible for readers to assess correctly the difficulties which attend collection even of the simplest and most innocent facts. I therefore propose to start by trying to explain the extraordinary state of affairs which prevails.

Foreigners in the U.S.S.R. may be divided into two entirely distinct categories—those who come on a short visit at the invitation of the Kremlin, and those resident within the country for a longer period by virtue of their duty or occupation. Of the former class I have already written a little. The principal characteristics of this class are their initial leanings towards the Left in politics, and the assiduous manner in which their hosts shepherd their every movement, so that they see just what the authorities wish them to see. It stands to reason that the Kremlin prefers to invite to Russia only those foreigners from whom they may expect sympathy and a tendency to see the best of conditions, rather than the worst. I do not remember a single foreign visitor of known Right Wing politics who visited Moscow as a guest of the Kremlin, or of any Russian organization, during my sojourn there, but there were many of the other political trend. It was pathetic for us who had lived there long enough to see below the surface to watch all these worthy men and women blissfully following the primrose path of pre-arranged visits and demonstrations, carefully staged for their benefit. 'There's none so blind as those who will not see.' Even when opportunity was placed before them, not one of these official visitors cared to probe behind the gilded façade and wander a little off the beaten and well-swept path. Several of our British visitors had ample leisure during their stay to make a little tour of the town, unaccompanied by Intourist or VOKS, with a member of our embassy to act as interpreter and guide. No attempt would have been made to influence their choice of route, or to push any particular exhibit before their eyes. They could have turned up any back street that they might happen to select, or visited any of Moscow's suburbs at random—a thing which they were certainly unable to do under the guidance of their official hosts. Perhaps they preferred not to risk disillusionment!

The foreign residents of more permanent standing are on quite a different footing. They are in Russia, not because they are thought to be sympathetic to Soviet ideals, but because their own respective governments have sent them to Russia to fill various appointments. They, therefore, are automatically regarded from the moment of their arrival, or long before it, with the most profound suspicion. Before the newcomer to Russia can start on his journey, application has to be made months in advance for an entry visa. This gives the authorities time to probe deeply into their records to find out whether anything is known against the intending visitor. Every foreigner, whether important or obscure, who has ever had dealings with Soviet officialdom, is bound to have a 'dossier' in his honour, reposing within the archives of the M.V.D. (see p. vii). Should anything be found recorded which is in the least degree 'unfavourable', the aspirant has about as much hope of getting into the U.S.S.R. as of getting to the moon.

Even if he is fortunate enough to pass this scrutiny, it does not mean that he is accepted as a man of goodwill or decent probity of conduct. All foreigners resident in Russia are regarded automatically as potential spies and are treated accordingly.

This applies particularly strongly, of course, to service attachés, but is not limited to them. General Seraev, the officer deputed to conduct all dealings with foreign service attachés, once told me quite frankly that every foreign service attaché, no matter how he conducted his life in Moscow, was regarded as a spy by the Soviet authorities. It can hardly be expected that a nation which has been caught disguising its own army officers as chauffeurs in its own embassies abroad will limit its suspicions only to those foreign diplomats who announce themselves openly as naval, military, or air officers. In fact, of course, they do not so limit their suspicions. Every foreigner, from an ambassador downward, from the first moment of his arrival in Russia is subjected to a special surveillance, which can hardly be credited unless it has actually been experienced.

The Russian people are by nature friendly, and would probably be hospitable if political and economic conditions allowed. As matters stand, however, they are not allowed to show even those small gestures of courtesy to strangers which, in other lands, pass as the hall-mark of a decent and cultured human being. Draconian laws are in force, forbidding any intercourse whatsoever between Soviet citizens and foreigners, except on strictly official affairs which must be approved and rigidly controlled by higher authority. Never once during my stay in Moscow did any Russian invite me to his home, nor did any Russian ever accept an invitation to my flat—exception in both cases being made for large official receptions, cocktail parties, and similar wholesale entertainment. Even at the big diplomatic receptions and official entertainments, only those Russians are permitted to attend who are detailed to do so as part of their duty. Even so they are not permitted to circulate freely among the other guests, but are watched by emissaries of the M.V.D. and sometimes shepherded into a corner or rounded up like a lot of children and taken home early, lest they should commit the gross indiscretion of behaving like a normal guest.

In the Soviet Zone of Germany, where the baneful influence of the M.V.D. is not so strongly felt, we occasionally managed to 'break the ice' slightly, and began to get on terms of common-sense friendship with a few of the Soviet officers with whom we had to deal. But they did not survive long to enjoy our friendship. In almost every case the same thing happened. Colonel X would one day fail to turn up, his place being taken by a new man, Colonel Y. To our tender enquiries concerning Colonel X we got nothing but an evasive answer. 'He has got another job.' We never saw or heard of any of our friends again after these disappearances.

In Moscow no Russian dared to take this risk, even to the extent of being normally polite to a foreigner. It was not I myself in particular who was picked out as being a sinister enemy of the Soviet Union. One and all, with the exception of representatives of the 'satellite' states, every member of the foreign diplomatic community in Moscow was similarly ostracized. Nor was this queer behaviour due to boorishness on the part of the Russians, for even here in Moscow, under the eyes of the M.V.D., most of us found that the ordinary simple Russian people, the non-official classes, if left to themselves, were as willing to be friendly as any other people all over the world. One little incident will illustrate this.

I had been for a walk in the suburbs, and boarded a tram-car at its terminus to get back to the city centre. About seven or eight people got in at the same place, all apparently workers from the same factory. They spotted my foreign accent at once, when I asked the conductress where I had to change trams, and at once they all gathered round and started a most friendly conversation. I told them, half-jokingly, that I was an Englishman, one of those dangerous people with whom they ought not to talk at all, but they waved this away, saying: 'That's all right. We all know one another here. The conductress too is a friend of ours.'

The conversation was not on a high level of intelligence, but quite harmless and naïve—the sort of questions were asked of me which one might ask of a visitor from Mars. It was obvious that none of these people had ever seen a foreigner before. It was all most friendly and rather pleasant. Suddenly the tram stopped, and quite a large number of new people got in. From that moment I was ignored just as though I had never been there at all.

The same thing held good in more remote country villages well off the beaten track. Here the people behaved in much the same way as peasants usually behave toward a stranger in all remote country districts. There was reserve and taciturnity, but no unfriendliness or suspicion. They were willing enough in these remote districts to carry on a conversation about simple things of the country —about the weather, the crops, or the abundance of game in the forests—or to tell me the way to the next village.

But in Moscow itself and its suburbs things were very different. With rare exceptions, such as my tram ride, no Soviet citizen would dare to be seen even talking for a moment to a foreigner. It was unsafe for a foreigner even to ask the way, for as like as not the Russian to whom the question was addressed would report the occurrence to the nearest policeman, in order to save himself from suspicion should the brief conversation have been observed. A demand for the foreigner's identity papers would immediately follow, and in most cases a long and annoying delay would ensue before he would be permitted to go on his way.

It can be taken for granted that every Russian servant or employee who is permitted by the Soviet authorities to work for a foreigner, or have dealings with a foreigner, is under orders to render regular reports concerning that foreigner to the M.V.D. It is extremely difficult for a foreigner who uses a car to dispense with the services of a Russian chauffeur, chiefly because the authorities see to it that the foreigner continually fails in his driving test till he is just about due to leave the country! It is simplicity itself, therefore, for the M.V.D. to keep a check on the movements of all foreigners who use their cars extensively for getting about. Walking in Moscow is so unpleasant

11

owing to the filth and roughness of the streets, the narrow-
ness of the pavements, and the jostling of unwashed
crowds, that comparatively few foreigners move far on
foot. The public transport services—trams, buses, trolley-
cars, and the 'Metro'—though plentiful and cheap, are
also grossly overcrowded. So the majority of foreign
residents move everywhere by car, and by so doing present
no problem at all to the M.V.D.

Occasionally, however, the authorities may have to deal
with a more eccentric type of foreigner, a man who actually enjoys walking for its own sake, a man who likes to
see a bit more of the country in which he is living that can
be seen from the windows of a car. I am afraid that I was
just such a man. As soon as I discovered (and it did not
take long to discover) that Soviet officialdom did not
intend to have any contacts with me whatsoever, I was
faced with two alternatives. I could either resign myself to
a pleasant but idle life of theatres, cocktail parties, the
ballet and the opera, never moving anywhere but in a car,
and never penetrating beyond the main streets and boulevards of Moscow. Or I could follow my own natural
inclinations, as I had done all my life in thirty or forty
other countries of the world. I could spend my time trying
to get to know and understand the real Russian people. I
could try to get about a bit on my own feet, and in public
transport, in order to see the real Russia which lay behind
the beautiful broad boulevards. I chose the second alternative.

As soon as I told a few of my friends of these ideas, they
did their best to dissuade me. I was bombarded with dire

warnings. Many others, I was told, had started with similar ideas, but all sooner or later had been forced to abandon their interest in the life of the Soviet people, and had been compelled to fall back on cocktail parties, the ballet, and the opera. I am afraid that these gloomy forebodings only strengthened my determination to see what I could.

This may sound obstinate or foolhardy. I still think it was quite a reasonable attitude to take. There seemed no reason to suppose *then* that the Soviet government had any cause to feel ashamed of what a foreigner might see, if he began to investigate the ordinary life of the people. In all other lands I had always found the authorities only too pleased to exhibit the social progress which they had accomplished. I knew from my year in the Soviet Zone of Germany that the Soviet authorities were intensely proud of the improvements wrought by Communism in the lives of the common people. It seemed only natural that they would be delighted to let a foreigner see for himself some of the signs of this increased happiness and comfort.

As soon as possible, therefore, in order to see as much as I could of the country before winter restricted movement, I began to explore the outer suburbs of Moscow, and occasionally wandered further afield, taking an electric train well out into the country and walking far from any motor road through the forests and fields, returning to my flat in time for an evening bath. It was a form of exercise and recreation which I had followed all my life, and there seemed no valid reason why I should

13

change it. What I saw on these rambles will be described in later chapters. I am only concerned at present with the effect of these habits of mine upon the mentality of Soviet officialdom.

I can now say with certainty, as the result of my own experiences, that the Soviet authorities do not like foreigners to wander on their own behind the scenes, even in peaceful country districts, where nothing of a secret military nature could by any stretch of imagination be said to exist. They dislike this so much that they are prepared to go to any lengths to prevent it. I do not attempt to explain this attitude. That is for them to do if they can, or for the admirers of Communism in this and many other countries, who profess to believe that the Soviet Union is a model country, an example to the world, something to be exhibited with honest pride to any interested foreigner. The indisputable fact remains. The foreigner in Russia wanders off the beaten track at his peril.

So much do the authorities detest foreigners trying to see the real life of the Soviet people, that they have evolved an elaborate technique to prevent this. It is based upon continual 'shadowing' or 'sleuthing' of all foreigners, backed, if necessary, by more drastic action.

It was not long before I found that strenuous efforts were being made to watch my every movement. Opposite my flat, whose entrance was in a cul-de-sac, there was a window in which a watcher sat, night and day, with a telephone beside him. There must have been a special posse of plain-clothes men on duty near by, for I usually

14

found one of them on my heels soon after I had set out. These men were either very badly trained or else it was a part of the game to let their presence be felt, for I had no difficulty at all in detecting their presence. In fact I soon got to know them by sight.

Those who have not been subjected to constant shadowing by sinister-looking individuals can have but little idea of the uncomfortable feeling it gives. It is quite possible that the moral effect of this may in itself have been sufficient to deter some people from further solitary walks. At any rate it was the exception for foreigners to wander very far from the beaten track. A few persisted in doing so, and found it a most interesting experience, but, in comparison with the total strength of the diplomatic community, their numbers were remarkably few. So it may well have been with definite intent to intimidate the would-be explorer that these sleuths frequently conducted their business in such a clumsy manner that a blind baby could scarcely have failed to observe them.

As soon as I discovered that this continual sleuthing was going on, I interviewed General Seraev, and asked him to define to me clearly to what extent foreigners were at liberty to go about on their own, and to stipulate what limits the authorities wished to place upon my movements. He assured me that there were no restrictions whatsoever, except of course that certain 'forbidden zones' existed, which, he stated, were quite easy to recognize, as they were clearly marked. I then told him about the sleuths who followed me everywhere. I said that if it happened to be the Soviet policy to escort foreigners everywhere, then

15

naturally I must comply with their system, but if this were so, I suggested, it would be far more satisfactory, both for me and my sleuths, that the thing should be done quite openly. If only the detective on duty could be ordered to report to me daily, I promised to give him an outline of my plans and proposed movements and, indeed, consult him regarding any proposed walk, so as to avoid any risk of going inadvertently into places where foreigners were not wanted. I pointed out that this method would be far more in keeping with the dignity of a great nation than the present underhand, childish, and rather clumsily conducted manœuvres; that it would be satisfactory to me, since I would then know exactly where I stood; and obviously it would make things much easier for the sleuths. General Seraev merely denied that any such sleuthing was going on.

Faced with this official denial, the choices before me were to succumb to the moral pressure of this constant shadowing and cease to wander off the beaten track, or to continue my walks and take no notice of my followers, or to evolve a technique for throwing the sleuths off my track whenever I wished to enjoy the pure country air, unspoilt by their rather sinister presence. I chose the third course. Indeed I had no compunction in doing this, since I had been officially informed by General Seraev that there were really no sleuths behind me at all! Taking his word as being the truth, I could only assume that the unpleasant-looking thugs who so often could be seen dodging behind trees, or, by an amazing coincidence, taking identically the same country walk as myself—these thugs could, I concluded, only be unauthorized persons of evil intent, since I had General Seraev's assurance that they had no official status. Indeed, on one occasion, my assistant and I were so persistently annoyed on a country walk by the clumsy prowlings of two of these gentry that, when we met an ordinary uniformed policeman, we laid in wait for our followers. When they came hurrying round the corner on our track we reported them to the uniformed 'bobby', and gave them in charge as being 'people behaving in a suspicious manner suggesting criminal intent'! Of course they had some secret sign whereby they overawed the simple constable, so they did not remain in his custody for long, but at least we felt that we had scored a slight moral victory. On our return to Moscow I reported the whole affair to General Seraev, as proof that he was mistaken about the non-existence of sleuths, but I never received any answer from him, not even a formal acknowledgement of my note.

The uninitiated reader may wonder why we did not merely shrug our shoulders and accept the presence of these sleuths as an unpleasant feature of an unpleasant country, and resign ourselves to having them always dogging our footsteps. The reason why this attitude could not be adopted was that individual life in Russia is not held in the same esteem as it is in more normal countries. To put the matter more bluntly, I had an uncomfortable feeling that the authorities might stick at *nothing* to eliminate a foreigner whom they considered a nuisance to themselves. I may perhaps have placed too low a value on Soviet respect for diplomatic decencies, but I had some cause for this scepticism as will be seen later (Chapter V). Having this feeling, it became a question either of giving up all further attempts to see the real life of Russia or else of devising methods for leaving these rather dangerous companions behind.

There was, of course, no question whatsoever of espionage in all this. Had there been legitimate military activities which the authorities might quite naturally wish to keep from the eyes of foreigners, it would have been a simple matter to restrict the movements of foreigners by official regulation. There were, indeed, as General Seraev mentioned, many 'forbidden areas' of considerable extent, into which, quite naturally, we did not attempt to penetrate. These areas were already sufficiently guarded by every known device of military security. This additional technique for discouragement of foreign movement—this sleuthing combined with intimidation, and followed up, if necessary, by violence—this technique was aimed, not at safeguarding military secrets, but at *preventing foreign eyes from seeing the real social conditions in the slums of Moscow and in the surrounding country*. If this is not the true object, then what else can the true object be? If taking an interest in living conditions of the working classes can be called espionage, then let villages and working-class suburbs be declared 'forbidden areas'. I know of no other country in the world where such things are treated as a state secret. Perhaps some admirer of the Soviet way of life can explain to us why this should be the case?

I do not think it wise to explain in detail the technique

18

which I used for ridding myself of my unwanted shadowers
whenever I wished to take a peaceful country walk alone.
Other foreigners may also get tired of this tiresome
company sometimes and desire to see for themselves how
the ordinary people really live. It would be a pity to spoil
the market. In a vast overcrowded city, where one has to
fight one's way through a scrum of other would-be
passengers before boarding a tram, or a train of the underground 'Metro', it may frequently happen that one's
sleuth gets left behind in the crush, or, alternatively, he
may battle his way on to the car or train, only to find that
the foreigner has unfortunately failed to get on board. My
conscience was quite clear. There could be no question of
'undiplomatic behaviour' in outwitting these stupid and
unwelcome companions, since I had it on the word of
General Seraev that these people had no official status,
and therefore had no right to follow innocent people
about on their lawful journeys.

After I had evolved this technique, and thus had enjoyed
nearly two months of unaccompanied wandering, it
became obvious that the authorities would not let the
matter rest there. If they were really determined to keep
foreigners within an invisible fence and prevent any
freedom of movement off the beaten track, it was certain
that they would soon proceed to sterner measures. They
did.

The next step was the fabrication of 'incidents', designed
for the dual purposes of (a) intimidating the venturesome
foreigner still further by showing him the absolute power
of the Soviet police system, and (b) making propaganda

19

for their own people to teach them what dangerous and sinister people foreigners were.

Two such incidents were concocted against me after I had been in the country for a few months, and several others misfired owing to bad staff-work. I think that it is worth-while describing these incidents, because they do help the reader to realize the complete grip which the M.V.D. enjoys over everything, including manipulation of the truth. But, as this chapter already holds too much about my own personal doings, I will postpone these adventures till a later chapter.

The facts about Soviet life and social conditions which I am about to record were collected in the course of these travels, on foot or by public transport, in the suburbs and slums of Moscow itself and the neighbouring country up to a distance of a hundred miles in all directions from the capital. Quite a lot could be seen in such an area, above all by getting about on foot, for the more interesting parts were often out of reach of any motorable road. Even in Moscow itself, he who only goes where a car will take him does not see much of the city, since in most of the outer suburbs the roads are too bad for anything but lorries with a very high clearance and very strong springs.

But, if you take a map of the U.S.S.R. and draw a circle round Moscow at a radius of a hundred miles, you will see that the area which I visited only represents a pin-point on the vast expanse of the U.S.S.R. The question naturally will leap to the minds of many readers, 'Why not have gone further afield?' Once more the answer is the

20

same—because the Soviet authorities intensely dislike foreigners seeing anything at all of their country, and so they have devised a most efficient technique for preventing this.

Theoretically one can travel out of Moscow by any one of four methods—by train, by car, by air, or by public steamer on the Moscow-Volga Canal. Unfortunately the last-named closed down for the winter before I had time to try it. Foreigners have somehow succeeded in making the trip as far as Gorki on the Volga, or even further, about seven hundred miles journey. I very much doubt whether it was done with the blessing and approval of the Soviet authorities, rather probably thanks to a slip on the part of the control arrangements, but at any rate it has been done, and without any harm either to the voyagers or to the Soviet state. But with this one exception, matters were so arranged that it was next thing to impossible for a foreigner to do a long journey of the sight-seeing type which everyone, without any underhand intent, would quite naturally like to do in any foreign country in which one may happen to be living.

Air travel is the easiest to achieve, provided that one has a strong *bona fide* reason for getting to some definite destination; but air travel hardly counts from the point of view of enabling the traveller to see anything at all of the life of the people and social conditions generally. Perhaps that may be why air travel is the only mode of travel regarding which the Soviet authorities occasionally relent.

In order to travel by train on a long-distance journey it is necessary to produce one's identity papers and an authority for the journey, issued by some appropriate government department. This, in the case of foreigners, may be Intourist or VOKS as the case may be, according to whether the foreigner is a general-purpose traveller, or an invited 'sympathizer', or a diplomat. In the case of service attachés, approval for the journey has to be given by the Ministry of the Armed Forces. I need hardly say that this approval is not easily obtained. During the whole time that I was in Moscow it was never once granted, to me or to any other service attaché, though frequently requested.

Since I left Russia, news has reached me that journeys to Stalingrad and one or two other selected places have been allowed. So far I have not heard details of the degree of liberty of movement permitted to the travellers in these cases, but I feel safe in hazarding a guess that they were not let out of sight of their Soviet escort, nor given a free hand to travel how they liked or to see what they liked of the country. I shall not be at all surprised to hear that they had to do the journey by air, as being the mode of travel by which one sees the least.

The ways of the Soviet authorities regarding the movement of foreigners are unpredictable and unaccountable. During the whole of my time in Moscow their policy was to impose no *official* restrictions at all, but at the same time they so arranged matters as to prevent foreigners from wandering off the beaten track except at risk of unpleasantness or worse. I now hear that they have at last issued an edict restricting the movements of foreigners *officially* to the immediate precincts of Moscow, but at the same time have permitted a limited number of special journeys to places much further afield than any foreigner has been permitted to go in recent years. One thing only is quite certain amid these changes of treatment; *there is no change whatever in the policy*. No matter what new rules may be published, no matter how warmly the Kremlin may appear to be inviting a limited amount of tourism, the effect will be exactly the same as before. The foreigner will not be permitted any true insight into the way of life of the civil population, their standard of living, their every-day problems, hopes, fears, worries and difficulties.

Besides the impossibility of purchasing a long-distance railway ticket without production of personal documents, the authorities have two other strings to their bow for preventing foreigners from journeying far from Moscow. There is the impossibility of engaging accommodation at hotels without again producing 'documenti'. The foreigner who has not gone through the correct channels (applying for accommodation many days in advance through Intourist) will be politely told that no accommodation is available. If he does follow the correct channels he will get nowhere at all! Finally, even if the foreigner decides to avoid this difficulty by sleeping in the country or on a bench in one of the parks, he will not be able to avoid the need for producing his 'documenti' for very long. Unless he carries all his baggage about with him permanently, he will have to show 'documenti' when he deposits any kit at a cloak-room. If, on the other hand, he carries it about with him, his movements will be automatically restricted by this encumbrance, and he will be so conspicuous that a demand for 'documenti' will be certain before he has gone very far.

During my stay in Russia several foreign diplomats did actually manage to board long-distance trains, and sometimes arrived at places at a considerable distance from Moscow. But this brief freedom was at once terminated immediately they were forced to buy a meal, or dispose temporarily of their baggage, or make some arrangement for passing the night. Any one of these things—in fact any action at all by foreigners, other than walking about and trying not to be conspicuous—inevitably ended in their being politely refused any kind of facilities either for staying in that town or continuing their journey. In most cases they were speedily provided with air transport straight back to Moscow and never allowed out of sight of plain-clothes men till they were safely aboard the Moscow-bound aeroplane.

If the foreigner tries to explore Russia in his own car the result is just as unsatisfactory. It is impossible to buy petrol anywhere outside Moscow without producing a paper authorizing the journey. A foreigner is thus restricted to going only as far as the petrol capacity of his car will carry him. If he plans to do an extra long journey, the fact that he has had his car filled to capacity will at once be reported to the M.V.D. by their spies working at the Moscow petrol pump, or by the foreigner's own chauffeur. Consequently he will not get very far.

During my last few weeks in Moscow, when I no longer cared what the authorities might think of me, I made a determined effort to see a bit further afield than the hundred miles round Moscow to which I had been, till then, restricted. I had my car filled with petrol by my A.D.C. in order to keep the chauffeur in ignorance as long as possible, and we laid in a stock of tinned food sufficient to keep us self-contained for several days. All was in vain. The M.V.D. failed indeed to find out in which direction I intended to go. But this did not inconvenience them in the least. They merely arranged police posts next day on *all* roads leading out of Moscow (there are only twelve that are fit for a car). These police posts had orders to stop my car and inform me that the road was closed for repair beyond that point. It did not matter in the least that the repair story was palpably a lie, and that other traffic was passing freely in each direction even as this lie was being told. The police did not worry whether their story was believed or not; nor did their masters who had posted them, and had put this lie into their mouths. Indeed one policeman, when I pointed out to him the incongruity of all this traffic on a road which (he assured me) was out of action only a kilometre or so ahead, replied bluntly: 'Well, all I know is that I have had orders to tell *you* that the road is closed for repairs'!

On that day we tried in turn eight out of the twelve motor roads radiating from Moscow. The same farce was repeated on each of them.

It is possible that the M.V.D. might on this occasion have done more than merely picket the twelve roads to turn me back—if only they had been able to find out in advance by which road I intended to travel. They

25

certainly made strenuous efforts to discover this. When the A.D.C. took the car to the garage for petrol he was engaged in friendly conversation by a couple of Russian workmen there, who did their best to extract this bit of information from him. Later that afternoon (the eve of our expedition) I happened to return to my flat unexpectedly early. As I opened the front door suddenly, I came upon one of the maids busy at the telephone. If she had kept her head, I might have noticed nothing wrong, for I had given them permission to use the 'phone. But her expression of guilt at my sudden entry gave her away. I therefore signed to her not to interrupt her conversation, and, instead of walking straight through to my bedroom, I picked up a paper and sat down in an arm-chair near the telephone. The poor girl's conversation continued somewhat as follows:

'Yes. I know. But I assure you that I am doing my best. He never says very much beforehand. This time he has said nothing at all. You had better ring off now. You are making things very uncomfortable for me. Very well. Yes, I will do my best.'

If she had said to me: 'Do you mind if I use your telephone to make my report to the M.V.D.?' she could not have made it more blatantly obvious. It was an unpleasant feeling to have such a nest of police spies among one's own staff, but one could not feel any personal animosity toward them, knowing, as we did, that they had no choice in the matter. Like all other Soviet citizens, they got their orders and had to obey, no matter how repugnant the work might be to their own better feelings.

26

It would be interesting to know with what purpose these efforts were made to discover *in advance* precise details of my movements. If the authorities merely wished to know exactly where my motoring tour had taken me, after the tour was over, they were already assured of this information in due course through the report of my Russian chauffeur. Even if they wished to keep a constant watch on my movements during the tour itself, they were already able to do this by means of the police car, equipped with wireless, which invariably shadowed my car whenever we drove outside the city. If they wished to prevent me from leaving the neighbourhood of Moscow at all, they could easily do so (as indeed they did) by the simple act of placing a police post on all twelve motorable roads. If any or all of these things covered the sum total of their intentions, they had no need to take any further action, such as they undoubtedly did take, to find out in advance by which route I intended to travel.

I must not ascribe to the M.V.D. motives or intentions which they may not have had at all, but certain facts cannot be denied. It is a fact that I had already been the victim of two pre-arranged 'incidents' (fully described in Chapter V). It is a fact that the second of these incidents involved personal violence to me in the presence of a whole village population. It is a fact that, in spite of these numerous witnesses, not one word of the true story of this affair was allowed by the M.V.D. to leak out.

It is also a fact that the authorities detest foreigners who try to study social conditions at first hand by getting about the country on their own, though they had not, in my day, the honesty to say so. Finally it is a fact that the Communist doctrine places a very low valuation upon the rights of an individual as compared to the welfare of the State.

It has been established again and again beyond any shadow of doubt that the Soviet State, or its minions the M.V.D., will stick at nothing in so far as concerns the lives or liberties of individual *Soviet citizens*, if the welfare of the state is deemed to be involved. Lenin himself has propounded with unmistakable emphasis the theory that circumstances may demand the extermination of an entire community for the good of the state or for the furtherance of the Communist cause.

It is one thing, however, to treat Soviet citizens, or the members of some subject race, in this unscrupulous manner. Surely it would be a very different matter when dealing with a foreign diplomat? I put this as a question, but I do not myself presume to give the answer.

All that I can say with certainty, from my own personal experience, is that respect for diplomatic immunity does not deter a Soviet minor official from inciting Soviet citizens to personal violence against a foreign diplomat. Nor does respect for justice or the truth deter the authorities from suppressing the truth about such an incident and inventing a fantastic story in its place. To what extremes this lack of scruple might be carried, when dealing with a foreign diplomat, nobody outside the Polit-Buro can give an authoritative opinion.

Though I may claim with justification to be a fairly prosaic chap, not usually given to 'vain imaginings', I must own that after the affair of Perlovka Woods (Chapter V) I no longer enjoyed that complete confidence in the traditional sanctity of diplomatic privilege which no doubt I ought to have felt. It may be that my uneasiness was quite unjustified. Matters such as this appear in rather a different light when out on a lonely walk in the country with several sinister individuals dogging one's footsteps! It should be remembered in extenuation of my lack of faith that I had already seen this diplomatic sanctity violently assaulted without subsequent redress or even apology.

At any rate, rightly or wrongly, I decided not to test Soviet scruples too highly, nor to put temptation in the way of those who had already proved to me how unscrupulous, violent, and untruthful they could be. I can well believe that such fears may seem groundless and far-fetched to those who still think of the Soviet Union as a normal civilized country. At the risk of reiteration I cannot emphasize too strongly that it cannot be regarded as a normal country. It is necessary to live for a period in the U.S.S.R. to realize fully the absolute grip which the police system holds over every aspect of human existence throughout that land. It is necessary, as a foreigner, to have experienced the high-handed methods of their police system (as exemplified by the closing of the twelve roads against me) to realize fully their complete contempt for the rights of foreign diplomats or the decencies of normal international courtesy.

The power of suppressing inconvenient facts is something that simply cannot be imagined unless one has

29

actually seen the system at work. What became of all the inhabitants of Goliyanovo (see Chapter V) who knew the true story of the Perlovka Woods affair? If they have been allowed to continue at liberty it is only because the authorities know that terror of the M.V.D. is sufficient to keep their mouths shut. Any witness about whose discretion there might be any doubt would simply disappear. Among the millions working as slaves in concentration camps there may well be many whose only crime consists in happening to be present when the M.V.D. were engaged upon affairs of state.

For all these reasons it seemed to me advisable not to assist the M.V.D. gratuitously in the preparation of still further 'incidents' by proclaiming my future movements publicly or by falling into any set routine. Against such an all-powerful body this frail precaution could not be expected to save me from petty and childish annoyances, but at least it gave me the comfort of feeling that preparation of more ambitious schemes might be rendered a trifle more difficult.

It cannot be too strongly emphasized that 'Truth' in the Soviet Union is a close prisoner of the M.V.D. The warped creature who shows herself to the outer world in the guise of 'Truth' is a debased and perverted slave of the M.V.D.

The police system of the U.S.S.R. is all-powerful, and its entire resources are used whenever necessary to prevent the foreign resident from seeing how the ordinary people live. What can be the true reason behind this detestation of the inquisitive foreigner? It is absurd to claim that it is merely the anxiety to protect military secrets from foreign espionage. If this be the reason, then the entire country-side outside Moscow's principal boulevards must be one vast military field of activity. What, if that is the case, becomes of Soviet protestations concerning their lack of warlike preparations? If, on the other hand, it is not on account of military secrets that the wandering foreigner is debarred from the suburbs, the slums, and the surrounding villages of Moscow, what are the dark secrets for whose protection the M.V.D. are prepared to go to such extremes?

We may take it for granted that it is *not* on account of military secrets. In spite of the deterrent efforts of the M.V.D. there were very few slums and suburbs of Moscow that I did not visit in the course of my walks. There were not many country districts within a hundred miles that I did not visit also on my longer country walks. I can vouch for the fact that outside 'prohibited areas' (which are many and well guarded) the bulk of this extensive suburban and rural area contains no other secret than the standard of living of its inhabitants, the ordinary working classes of the U.S.S.R. Can this be the secret which the Kremlin wishes to hide from the outer world? Is it to prevent disclosure of such facts as will appear in subsequent chapters that the authorities carry out this childish 'sleuthing' and intimidation of foreigners? Is it to keep such facts from the world that they are prepared to mobilize the resources of M.V.D., the ordinary police, innumerable plain-clothes men and women, and such organizations as Intourist and the transport and hotel services?

31

Or can it be in order to prevent their own people from talking to foreigners, and thus gradually finding out the truth about the outer world? Whichever of these two reasons may be the true one (or perhaps both may be equally true), it would be interesting to hear a member of the Soviet government explaining the matter to one of our own Communists. Of what is the Soviet government ashamed? Why does it try to keep the resident foreigner penned within a wall of isolation?

CHAPTER III

GENERAL CONDITIONS

THE city of Moscow resembles in plan a spider's web, with the Kremlin in the centre. Twelve broad streets radiate from the Kremlin, and these are crossed at distances of about half a mile and a mile from the centre by two broad circular boulevards. It is also intersected roughly into two equal parts by the Moskva River, which wanders across the city in a series of pronounced loops and curves, and passes immediately along the South face of the Kremlin.

The Kremlin itself is a 'city within a city'. Within its massive mediaeval walls there are five large churches (none of which is used for worship now) and a large number of palaces and minor government buildings. It has its own shops, to which only specially privileged members of the upper hierarchy are admitted.

No unauthorized person is allowed to enter the gates of the Kremlin. It is impossible even to approach the gates without one's identity papers being demanded and one's business investigated. It is possible, once during one's sojourn in Moscow, to take part in a personally-conducted tour of certain parts of the citadel, but strong precautions are taken to ensure that no member of the party strays from the fold.

Extensive though the area of the Kremlin is, there is not sufficient accommodation within its walls for the fifty or more ministries of the Soviet Government. The 'Whitehall'

area of the capital spreads over the north-eastern neighbourhood of the Kremlin to a distance of nearly a mile.
Here also are to be found most of the theatres, all the big
cosmopolitan hotels, the best shopping streets, and the
Lubianka Prison. Flanking the Kremlin's eastern wall lies
also the famous Red Square, containing the tomb of
Lenin, in front of which take place the great parades of
Labour Day and other important dates of the Communist
calendar.

At the risk of seeming to be writing a guide-book I have
started this chapter with a brief topographical outline,
because what I have just described is about the only
portion of Moscow that many foreign visitors ever see.
The outer of the two broad circular boulevards, the
'Sadovia', has the makings of a very beautiful and dignified
street, worthy of any great capital. Its northern stretches
are in good condition, smoothly surfaced and flanked for
the most part by imposing façades. This is the portion over
which the newly arrived foreigner will usually drive to his
hotel, if he comes to Moscow by train. It is calculated to
give the newcomer a favourable first impression of the
city. The southern portion of this same great circular
boulevard, beyond the Moskva River, is rather a different
story, but this does not matter very much, as the foreign
visitor on a short tour is unlikely to go there.

Similarly the south-western boulevard, leading out to
the civil airport of Vnukovo, is by far the finest, cleanest,
and architecturally most presentable of all the radiating
boulevards. The Moscow City Soviet certainly has a flair
for showmanship. It is quite possible to spend a few days

34

in the capital, especially if one is personally conducted everywhere by kind Soviet hosts, and still go away with feelings of respect and admiration for all that one has seen.

Within a week of my arrival I decided to explore on foot some of the narrower streets leading off the 'Sadovia'. As I turned off this fine street up the first minor street, picked at random, it was like stepping straight from a modern European city into the slums of a backward Eastern town. The surfaces of all the back streets are partially cobbled and partially unmetalled mud. With few exceptions they are quite unfit for any motor traffic other than Russian lorries with a very high 'clearance'. The pavements are narrow or non-existent, and full of pot-holes and large muddy puddles. The imposing stone façades of the 'Sadovia' are replaced at once by dilapidated factories and ancient wooden hovels. On all these buildings there is a marked absence of paint.

The windows of these wooden hovels, the dwellings of the workers, look as though they have never been cleaned and never opened. Now and then an open door may give a glimpse into the interior of one of these drab and tumble-down shanties. The interior is dark and forbidding, for the windows are so small and so thickly encrusted with the grime of ages as to be almost useless. Even when electric lights are left on in broad daylight, which usually seems to be necessary in these murky interiors, the candle-power seems too feeble to make much impression on the foetid haze within. There is a constant coming and going of inmates. It seems almost impossible that so many people

35

can find room to breathe in such restricted accommodation.

These ancient wooden houses are not as a rule built on any regular pattern or in unbroken rows. There are numerous alleys and courtyards, and in these the filth is often indescribable. It must not be imagined now that I am writing of some one particularly obnoxious slum. These conditions are fairly general throughout the back streets, even immediately adjacent to the civilized shopping centres. I know one particular courtyard, for example, within five minutes' walk of the Kremlin and of the Bolshoi theatre, where the tenants of neighbouring houses have to wade ankle deep through garbage and human excreta in order to reach their homes.

The streets themselves are almost as filthy, though here the more unpleasant items get fairly quickly covered by the all-pervading mud. For in most of these narrow back streets there is a constant stream of lorry traffic, hooting its way vociferously through dense jostling masses of pedestrians for whom there is no room on the pavements, covering them with mud from head to feet. Everything, from the houses themselves to the people, is covered with a dingy grey-brown film of mud or dust.

Moscow is grossly overcrowded. Even in the better parts accommodation is allotted according to standards which would not be tolerated by the health authorities of a Western town. I had a flat just sufficiently big to house my A.D.C. and myself in accordance with reasonable, but by no means lavish, Western ideas of comfort. On the floor below me, in another flat of the same dimensions, seven families were living—a total of about thirty to thirty-five people in all. These were not workers of the poorest classes but artisans and minor officials.

On one occasion I was given an opportunity to look inside a typical 'factory dormitory', where unmarried workers of both sexes are customarily accommodated. It was in the basement of the factory under one of the machine-shops, and was ordinarily occupied by the shift off duty while the machinery continued to throb ceaselessly over their heads. The dormitory consisted of a long narrow cellar, so thickly crammed with beds that there was no room to stand between two beds unless one placed one's feet toe to heel, one behind the other. The linen on the beds was grey with age and grime. There was no hanging space or storage space where individuals could place their discarded clothing, but I gathered that this did not matter because the average Russian does not take off many clothes to go to bed. The windows were like those of the wooden hovels already described, small, hermetically sealed, and caked with cobwebs and grime. Though they were set high in the walls of the dormitory, they were still below street level outside, so that the most one could have seen, if the glass had been sufficiently transparent, would have been the legs of passers-by up to the knees. The stale stench of humanity was so overpowering that I was not able to remain there long.

Industrialism and oriental backwardness and primitiveness are closely intermingled throughout the back regions of Moscow, even quite close to the centre. But conditions naturally tend to get worse as one penetrates the outer suburbs. Here one finds a labyrinth of railways sprinkled with factories, power stations, and untidy acres of derelict ground, strewn with dumps of rusty machinery, or factory refuse, or stacks of timber and coal. In these outer suburbs the state of the roads becomes unbelievably bad. I have seen lorries, even with the high clearance that is a match for most ruts and pot-holes, sometimes completely bogged in one of these suburban streets.

In most great cities of the world there are slums which are a disgrace to humanity, and it may be thought by some that I have purposely picked one or two of Moscow's particularly bad spots in order to paint a gloomy picture. This is definitely not the case. One of the results of Communism in practice is that it reduces everything except the privileges of the official classes to the same dead level. In Moscow there are no select residential suburbs, such as will be found in most 'capitalist' cities. All suburbs, indeed all parts of the town that lie off the principal boulevards, are in general terms as I have described above. It is true that there are, out in the country twenty or thirty miles from the capital, certain rural residential areas, where the really big men of the Communist hierarchy have their *dachas*—pleasant country villas, each one set in its own wooded estate, surrounded by a high wooden paling and guarded by a police cordon. But such joys are only for the chosen few. For the vast mass of city and suburban workers there is a dead level of dingy squalor, with overcrowding in their homes, in the streets, and above all in the public transport services, and with no means of escape from the ever-present dreariness of the industrialism to which they are bound.

One cannot escape the impression that in these suburban communities the factory is what matters; the individual counts for nothing at all. As long as the streets are fit to carry the factory traffic of heavy lorries, nobody seems to mind if the tired worker has to trudge through a mile or more of mud and slush to the nearest tram-line, because the roads are too bad to take a passenger bus. There are comparatively few streets in the outer suburbs of Moscow which can be reached without a long walk from the nearest tram-line. This was the method by which, sector by sector, I gradually explored most of the city and its surroundings.

The public transport services are on the whole good, if judged by other local standards, but in quantity are totally inadequate for the needs of the population. Travel is amazingly cheap. It is possible, for example, to get from one side of the capital to the other for fifteen kopeks if you go by tram. This is about a penny by the normal rate of exchange. Public transport consists of trams, buses, trolley-buses, the 'Metro' (underground railway), and so-called 'fixed-route taxis'. Of these forms of transport only the trams, as I have just explained, are of much practical service to suburban dwellers off the few radiating high roads. There are only twelve of these roads out of Moscow fit for wheeled motor traffic, so the buses, trolley-buses, and 'fixed-route taxis' are restricted to these twelve routes. It can be appreciated that very large areas of dwellings lie between, and in some cases lie very far from any of these arterial roads.

The 'Metro' is quite good, and surprisingly clean. It is

39

the civic pride of Moscow. Its stations are very fine architectural masterpieces, constructed mainly in marble. The carriages are clean, and the service is quick and efficient. But at present there are only three lines, each running across the city from suburb to suburb. There is no proper correspondence between these three lines. They intersect roughly in the vicinity of the Kremlin, but have no junction stations. Consequently the 'Metro', good and efficient as it is, does not help greatly to solve the main transport problems of large parts of the city.

Every form of public transport is overcrowded to a degree almost incredible by normal standards. Almost every tram has got passengers clinging precariously to the outside, even in the bitterest winter weather. The buses and trolley-buses would have the same, were it not for the fact that there is nothing to cling to when their doors are shut. Even these vehicles, however, usually have several small boys riding on the bumpers at the back.

In remarking, a few paragraphs back, that Communism reduces everything to the same dead level, I do not want to give the impression that it produces social equality. There is a dead level of drabness and squalor which pervades all strata of society—their homes, their clothing, and above all the residential areas in which they live—but within this dead level of drab monotony, from which nobody escapes, there are degrees of comfort and discomfort. There are, for example, in some of the outer suburbs, modern multi-storied flats, either recently finished or still under construction. These are said to be the future homes of the workers, but it will be very many years before the average working-class family finds a home in one of these modern buildings. At present those which are ready for occupation are inhabited by the families of petty officialdom—junior officers of the fighting services, minor party officials, and some of the higher technical and administrative staffs of factories and public services. Even these favoured classes are grossly overcrowded like everyone else in Moscow. As I never had the privilege of an invitation to enter one of these tenements, it was only possible to get some idea of the number of inhabitants by a combination of three methods—by watching the constant flow of inmates in and out of the building, by noting what proportion of the total windows were illuminated at night, and by observing the quantity and quality of the laundry which the inhabitants festooned about the building. This last gave a good indication, not only of the numbers of inmates but also of their social status and culture! Judged by these three standards, little doubt remained that, even in these superior dwellings, slum conditions are prevalent.

Apropos of lights in windows, it is interesting to note that all houses in Moscow, with practically no exception, show lights from every window after dark. This seems to indicate that every room is both a living room by day and a bedroom by night. There is no space in overcrowded Moscow for the luxury of eating and sleeping in separate rooms.

It goes without saying that in these ant-like conditions, where several families may have to share a room, there can be no privacy for families or individuals. This is quite in accordance with the Communist view of life, so it naturally does not worry the authorities. Their primary concern is to crowd as many workers as possible into the immediate neighbourhood of the factories where they work. The less privacy and family life there is, the more workers of both sexes will be available for industry. Everything is done to break down the idea of family, so that the mothers as well as the fathers will be available to spend the whole of their working days in the factories. There are communal eating-houses, communal bath-houses, crêches for the infants, and 'Pioneer houses' (Boy Scout and Girl Guide centres). There are workers' clubs and *Agitpunkts* (of which more later) so that adolescent youths and young girls need not spend such meagre spare time as they may get in their dreary and overcrowded 'homes'.

Though the central part of Moscow, near the Kremlin, is fairly symmetrical in plan, the outer suburbs seem to have spread themselves haphazard far into the surrounding country. Along the twelve radial roads, fit for motor traffic, 'ribbon development' has ranged far afield, but between these ugly extensions of the city, suburbia (or rather slum-dom, for in Moscow both are one) merges imperceptibly into a flat and industrialized countryside. The villages near Moscow are like suburban slums. The suburban slums are like overgrown villages in their lack of elementary drainage, sanitation, and other normal civic amenities. For many miles out—as far as one can go, in fact, by the ordinary tram or bus services—the same dismal aspect is to be found—i.e. clumps of drab overcrowded dwellings centred round a factory or group of factories. It is only when you take one of the electric trains or a long-distance bus, and go fifty to a hundred miles out of the capital, that you get into the real unspoiled country and see the old village life of Russia as it still is, when unspoiled by Communist industrialism.

For it is the impact of Communist industrialism upon an eastern peasant population which has produced the foul social conditions to be seen in and round Moscow today. In small village communities with an oriental standard of living, lack of sanitation, lack of decent housing, lack of roads—none of these matter very much, because the ways of the people are simple and their wants are few. But if one tries to run a great city of several millions on the same primitive lines as an oriental village, the result is bound to be rather an eyesore, particularly if the civic ideals of those in power do not rise higher than 'shop-window dressing' for the benefit of the superficial observer, and if in the background there is merely the harsh material aim of turning the city into a vast dormitory for as large an industrial proletariat as possible.

Such attempts as have been made to beautify the city and its surroundings only serve to enhance the prevailing atmosphere of drab ugliness. There are so-called 'Parks of Culture and Rest' in which the workers are supposed to find solace, mental refreshment, and relaxation. There are several of these parks dotted about the suburbs. Apart from the fact that there are trees, which no human effort can uglify, these parks are pathetic monuments to what is believed by the rulers of Russia to constitute proletarian

43

happiness. In the more frequented parts near the main entrances the eye is tormented by huge red slogans proclaiming the Communist faith and by crude statues of Lenin and Stalin. Blaring radio loudspeakers pour forth an endless stream of propaganda.

If you go deeper into the park to escape these entertainments you find a wilderness of neglect and dirt. You may get out of earshot of the radio, and you may get out of sight of the red slogans, but you are unlikely to escape the statues. If you sit for a while on a seat in these more secluded parts, it will not be long before you perceive a watcher, peering furtively at you from behind a tree, in case you may be keeping a secret rendezvous.

In short, one cannot escape, anywhere in Moscow, from the ubiquitous air of dreary sadness and ugliness—squalid neglect in the buildings, roads and parks, depressing ugliness in the dress and appearance of the people. Even in the better shopping centres one never sees a decently-dressed man or woman. One never sees a smiling or cheerful face, except among small children.

Mention of the 'better shopping centres' brings me to the question of standards of living. What can the ordinary workers buy with their wages?

Any economic study of social life in Russia is liable to be rendered out of date by sudden changes in economic policy. I can only write of conditions as they were a few months ago. When I first got to Russia in 1947, there was an elaborate system of rationing in force, far more elaborate than anything to be found in other countries. Not only were there coupons for a great variety of foods and commodities, but these ration scales were graded in accordance with the importance of the work which each individual might be doing for the State. Those who were too ill or too old to work got nothing at all, and were dependent upon charity or the kindness of friends or relations. In addition to this grading of ration scales there was a further grading in favour of the more privileged members of the hierarchy by means of special shops, into which only certain people were allowed to go. The commodities displayed for sale in these special shops bore no resemblance whatsoever to the shoddy stuff to be obtained in ordinary 'non-privileged' shops.

In December, 1947, however, with a great flourish of propaganda trumpets, the whole of this system of rationing was abolished. Henceforward, it was decreed, there should be no more special shops for privileged customers. There should be no more coupons. Everyone was to be free to buy what he liked and where he liked. This sounded magnificent 'on paper', but in actual fact it has made practically no difference at all to the welfare of the poorer unprivileged classes. It seems very doubtful whether it was ever intended to make any real difference.

When I left Russia in June, 1948, the situation was roughly as follows. There was still a world of difference in the quality and quantity of supplies and stock to be found in the better shops of the centre, as compared with the shops of the poorer outlying suburbs. Owing to the rigid control over all visitors to the Kremlin, which I have mentioned earlier, it was never possible to investigate the quality and quantity of the goods to be purchased at shops

45

within the Kremlin. Needless to say, it would be only a few officials who would enjoy the opportunity of patronizing those shops.

Outside the Kremlin, in the civilized centre of the city it was *theoretically* possible for any inhabitant of Moscow to do his or her shopping. Yet every day vast queues could be seen lining up outside the much inferior shops of the outer suburbs, where the commodities to be obtained were still as poor in quality and as scanty in quantity as ever. Why was this? Why did not the poorer people avail themselves of their theoretically new-found freedom to shop in the most favourable places? The answer is to be found in two factors—lack of spare time and lack of adequate public transport facilities.

It is still quite impracticable for the great mass of housewives, living in the outer industrial suburbs, to come into the centre of the city for their daily shopping. Cheap as public transport may be, it is still too expensive to be used extensively as a daily routine by the poorest classes, and, in any case, too much time would have to be spent in battling with crowds on the trams or 'Metro'. So in practice the good well-stocked shops of the centre are still preserved for the patronage of those who live and work near the governmental centre of the city, for the vast army of bureaucrats and minor party officials and their wives. It is very easy for the government, which retains tight control of the whole service of retail distribution, to ensure that the favoured shops of the centre get the 'plums' of everything and that the shops in the outer wilderness get the dregs.

46

An example of how this system of discrimination works can be found by studying the vicissitudes of the staple commodity, bread. Soon after the decree abolishing rationing was published, it began to be clear that one of its effects was a serious increase in the size of the daily queues outside baker's shops. For a while this was explained away by saying that the poor people were at last able to buy white bread instead of black for the first time for many years, and that there was rather a rush to purchase this new luxury. But before long this theory was proved to be false. Women were to be seen coming away from these queues carrying *black* bread, not white. At the same time it was found to be quite easy to buy white bread in baker's shops nearer the centre of the city, without standing in a queue at all. It was obvious that stocks of bread varied greatly as between the 'better' shops of the centre and the small baker's shops of the outer regions. Matters became so bad during the worst phase of the transition period (following the abolition of rationing) that in some districts housewives had to queue all night long in the snow to get their daily pittance of bread for the following day.

We in this country already know some of the curious effects which can be caused by governmental control of the distribution of food supplies. There have been cases in our own country where one particular region is well supplied with some commodity, even to superfluity, while in another part the same item cannot be bought for love or money. But in our country the actual retail trade to the customer is still in the hands of a private firm or dealer. It is up to the firm, or its customers, to complain if they

47

find that they are being left out of a fair distribution of various available commodities. Not so in the Soviet Union. There the whole chain of transactions, down to and including the retail sale to the customer, is in the hands of bureaucracy. There are no private traders, except to a very limited extent in the markets. What is more important still, there is no customer who would dare to express dissatisfaction with the quality or quantity of goods available for purchase in the local shop. There is no such thing as an informed and active and fearless public opinion, such as there still is (thank God) in our own country, to expose 'rackets' and public scandals of this kind, whether they be due to bureaucratic inefficiency or to a more deliberate intent to cheat the unprivileged classes for the benefit of those favoured by the government.

In Russia, as I hope to show in the next chapter, there is no such thing as a free public opinion. It is extremely doubtful whether the poor housewives of the outer slums even realize that there are better things to be bought in the superior shops of the centre. They never have time to go there to see for themselves, and it would be an unusually bold and foolhardy journalist who would risk his own liberty by drawing attention to this anomaly.

In the poorer outer suburbs shops are mainly limited to the baker's shop and two kinds of general stores, one for foodstuffs (known as a 'Gastronom') and the other for other consumer goods. All, of course, are governmentally run, or at any rate run by official organizations such as the local Soviet or the factory committee. There is no redress for the dissatisfied customer, such as the ability to take his or her custom elsewhere. They have to take what they can get without a murmur.

It is unnecessary, I think, to give the reader complicated tables showing in roubles the wages earned by various types of worker, and comparing these with the current prices of all sorts of food and consumer goods. In a normal country, where the worker has sufficient leisure time and freedom of travel to take his money to the best market, there may be great value in comparative tables of that kind for assessing the standard of living. But in the U.S.S.R. such figures would be meaningless. The hard fact remains that, in spite of the much publicized abolition of rationing and controls, the poorer working classes can still purchase practically nothing that makes life worth living. The practical proof of this is to look at them as they go about their daily drudgery, clad in old rags which must have seen service for generations, their faces listless and expressionless with that peculiar texture of transparent lead which indicates a life spent much too near the starvation line. One has only to compare these depressed wretches with the robust and often plump appearance of Soviet officialdom in all its grades to realize that, in a land where the state is all-powerful, a mere paper decree on abolition of preferential rationing can mean in actual practice exactly what the authorities intend it to mean and nothing more.

Truth herself is a slave and close prisoner of the M.V.D. I will now try to explain how this is accomplished.

49

CHAPTER IV

TRUTH IN THE U.S.S.R.

ONE of the proudest boasts of the present régime is that it has almost entirely abolished illiteracy among its people. It is a boast which is justified and it is certainly a very remarkable achievement. It is only when one begins to look into the motives which may have inspired this great reform that admiration for the philanthropy of the Kremlin becomes tinged with doubt. The value of being able to read depends almost entirely upon what one can read. The mere ability to read, without the ability to form one's own independent opinion on what one has read, can be a powerful mental chain to bind the reader to the will of those who provide the reading material.

The recently illiterate population of the U.S.S.R. is like a child with a new toy. Soviet citizens have become indefatigable readers. Their minds have not been expanded by broad and true education to be able to use this new trick of reading with discretion and judgement. Reading has gone to their heads. They are intoxicated with the sudden excitement of being able to understand the printed word. Their simple minds have hardly yet had time to attune themselves to the fact that it is just as easy to lie in print as with the tongue. Till quite recently they were ready to accept anything which appeared in print as being almost a sacred truth. This attitude is changing slowly, for not even the most trusting of readers could continue for ever to swallow some of the statements and counter-statements which have been published in the Russian language during the past few years.

At the same time it must be accepted that the propagandists of the Kremlin at present possess, and will continue to possess, till they blunt it by their own stupidity, a weapon of tremendous power in the fact that they alone have access to this enormous reading public, and the fact that this public is still almost incredibly gullible. Not a single printed word can reach the people of the Soviet Union unless it emanates from printing presses of the Soviet government. This applies not only to newspapers but to books on every conceivable subject. It even applies to theatre programmes.

Soon after getting to Moscow I bought myself a few of the ordinary elementary text-books, used in children's schools, in order to find out for myself what sort of a mental picture of our world was being given to the rising generation of Soviet citizens. It is hard to believe that these books purport to be describing the same world that we know, or the events of history which most of us have been taught. Astonishment passes all bounds when one reads the official Soviet version of certain very recent events, which many of us know by personal experience to have happened in quite a different manner to that taught by the Kremlin. As one example out of many, the following is a close translation of some passages from a 'History of the U.S.S.R. (Short Course) edited by Professor A. V. Shestakov'. These passages purport to describe the early events of the Second World War.

'During the war unity was born between all the freedom-loving peoples of the world. Alliance and friendship between the U.S.S.R. and Great Britain and the United States was consolidated. At first England and the United States were not ready for war. They needed time to collect and prepare their forces. The Soviet Union drew upon herself alone almost all the blows of the enemy, and with her own blood saved not only herself but her allies.'

The 'war' which this account describes is the 'Great Fatherland War', which began for Russia on the 22nd June, 1941, when the Third Reich suddenly assaulted Russia, in spite of the treaty which Hitler and Stalin had signed between them. The fact that the British Empire had already been 'drawing upon herself alone all the blows of the enemy' for *nearly two years before Russia was forced unwillingly into the contest* is conveniently and adroitly slurred over. The aggressions of Russia against Eastern Poland and the three Baltic republics are turned by the Professor into a large-hearted movement by the Red Army to rescue the people of these lands from the 'Fascist hordes' of Germany. In similar vein the war against Japan is dismissed as a troublesome affair between Japan and China, which the U.S.S.R. finally assisted the U.S.A. and Great Britain to settle quickly in order to restore peace to the world. As in the case of the war with Germany, so with the war against Japan. There is no hint in this school text-book that the British Commonwealth of Nations and the United States of America had already got the Japanese on the run after several years' hard fighting when the Soviet Union chipped into this war for the last fortnight or so. There is no mention of any such factor as the atomic bomb.

In short, this little text-book throughout its pages is a shining example of the art of presenting history in a form which suits the sponsors of the book. The pages dealing with Marshal Stalin's non-aggression pact with Hitler, with the Soviet invasion of Finland, and the early days of the German assault on Russia are real masterpieces in the art of juggling with awkward facts. The paragraph dealing with the Finnish war is, I think, well worth quoting in full as an illustration of how the truth can be handled by real experts on propaganda.

'A frightful menace hung over Leningrad. The great city was almost on the very frontier of Finland. In Finland the Fascists were in power. They had visions of seizing Leningrad and other Soviet territory by force, and plotted a war with us. The Red Army dug its way through impregnable Finnish defences and dealt the Finns a shattering blow. The frontier was pushed back from Leningrad.' Thus in a few carefully chosen words a cynical act of aggression against a small peace-loving country (an act of aggression which shocked the world already hardened to such crimes by the deeds of Mussolini in Abyssinia and Hitler in Europe) is presented to the rising generation of Russia as an unavoidable act of self-defence, undertaken most unwillingly by a great peace-loving and benevolent power!

So it goes all through the school text-books of the U.S.S.R. It is probably fairly safe to say that there is not a sentence printed in any school text-book which has not first been carefully vetted by the propaganda experts. It is hardly surprising that the younger generations leave school implicitly believing exactly what the Kremlin would have them believe. It is not surprising that each new generation produces a fine crop of ardent young Komsomols (budding young Communists) to swell the ranks of the Party and to furnish large numbers of loyal and unquestioning 'yes men' and 'yes-women' to fill the minor bureaucratic posts of the great governmental machine.

Not only at school is this indoctrination carried out. In the 'Pioneers' (a perverted imitation of our Boy Scouts and Girl Guides) every child is taught from infancy the correct code of behaviour for a good Soviet citizen. They are taught above all things the virtue of 'healthy suspicion', by which term the Soviet religion describes the attitude of constant watchfulness against anything which may seem to be contrary to Communist doctrine and policy. Little children, who in other lands would be just about learning to say their prayers at their mother's knee, are taught here to watch their own parents for any sign of 'deviation', and if necessary to denounce their parents to the M.V.D. They are taught to note any stranger passing near their homes, and report him at once to the police. One of the saddest experiences for a foreigner in Russia who is genuinely fond of children is to notice the sinister change which comes over them as this teaching begins to have its effect.

At the age of fourteen those selected for outstanding Communist zeal and loyalty are permitted to continue this early 'Pioneer' training in the ranks of the Komsomols. Those who are so selected now become prospective candidates for eventual admission into the Communist Party. The word *Komsomol* is an abbreviation for 'Young Communist League', the actual members being strictly speaking called in Russian '*Komsolmoltzi*'. As its name implies, this organization is a breeding ground or recruiting-zone for the Communist Party and a means of keeping loyalty to the Party alive within the youth of the country. It has its own newspaper. It is regarded as a *corps d'élite*, expulsion from which would be regarded by young Russians as social death.

Membership entails unquestioning obedience to the orders of the Party. The period of test for novitiates is extremely severe. They are purposely given most arduous and frequently repulsive jobs to test their sincerity and zeal. They are expected to stand out *vis-à-vis* the older generations as shining examples of Communist ardour. The Kremlin sets very great store by this constant boosting by the younger enthusiasts of what otherwise might become the flagging ardour of those whose ripening years are beginning to bring disillusionment.

But the propaganda machine does not, of course, content itself with tackling the pliable minds of adolescence and youth. This is the great value of complete literacy among the population. Soviet citizens can continue to be impregnated with propaganda long after they have left school—in fact all their lives.

There are two principal daily papers in Moscow, *Pravda* (which means 'Truth') and *Izvestia* (which means 'Information'). It is perhaps a healthy sign of dawning scepticism that one often hears sly jokes from more daring Russians to the effect that these papers are alike in being full of '*izvestia*' which is never '*pravda*'. It takes courage and considerable provocation to make such jokes in the U.S.S.R. For these two papers are the official mouth-pieces of the Communist Party and of the Government respectively.

There is no excuse for any citizen not to read these papers daily, because there are hoardings all over the town on which both papers are affixed for perusal by all who cannot afford a paper of their own. Other papers also are displayed on public hoardings—notably *Trud* ('Labour') and the *Literary Gazette*. The latter, in spite of its cultured name, has little to do with literature or culture of any kind. It is merely an extremely scurrilous rag, mainly devoted to publication of virulent attacks upon prominent or temporarily prominent foreigners.

It is interesting to note the amount of time devoted by the average citizen to the reading of these freely exhibited papers. It is unusual to see anybody devoting more than a rapid glance at the front pages of *Pravda* or *Izvestia*, for as a rule these pages are wholly occupied by open letters from the workers of this or that factory to 'Our glorious leader, Comrade Stalin', testifying in the most fulsome terms of adulation the undying loyalty of the workers and their unswerving determination to carry out his Five Year Plan in four years or less. Even the docile Soviet public seems to have had about enough of that sort of stuff. Unless a policeman is standing near, the average reader usually takes all that as read, and passes on quickly to something a trifle more interesting in the back pages.

But the tragedy of it all is that, no matter what he reads, propaganda oozes from every printed word, perhaps not quite so crudely and blatantly as in the 'letters from loyal workers' but all the more insidiously for being served up in palatable form. It goes without saying that nothing whatsoever in international news is reported in the Soviet press without being given an anti-foreign or rather anti-Western twist. Sometimes it is cleverly done, and at other times very clumsily, but the cumulative effect of all this ceaseless reiteration cannot fail to leave its mark.

It must be remembered that the Soviet citizen has no other source of information to which he can turn to counterbalance the trend of thought cultivated by the government-run newspapers. It is not possible in the U.S.S.R. for any writer to express his own point of view on any subject whatsoever. Even such completely non-controversial subjects as science or the arts come under the sway of the propaganda machine. It is not even a case of each writer publishing at his own peril, and being liable to be brought to account for any unacceptable views. The whole machinery is entirely in governmental hands. It is impossible for anything to get into print at all, unless it originates from the government or from a governmentally-inspired source.

An astonishing example of this control occurred shortly before I left Moscow, when certain musical composers and dramatists of unassailable talent and repute were publicly pilloried by the Soviet press for something described as 'formalism'. This new word in the jargon of Communism apparently stigmatizes any expression of art that fails to teach the audience the essential truths of Marxism, Leninism, and Stalinism. Certain plays and other performances

57

were banned, even though a year or less ago they had been performed with every sign of approbation by the great ones of Moscow. That did not matter. This new crime of 'formalism' had been discovered since those days. Eventually the men of art who were thus pilloried made a public confession of their crime of 'formalism', and promised only to produce in future art which conformed to the ideals of Communism, and which preached its doctrine.

Thus mentally there is no escape whatever now for the man or woman of Russia from the constant drip of propaganda. In this respect the Kremlin has out-goebbeled Goebbels. For even in the most hectic days of Nazi propaganda it was still possible for the ordinary German to forget it all for a short while and seek relief in the pure art of the old pre-Nazi masters of music. In the Soviet Union there is no such thing as 'pure' art. There is, in the official view of the Kremlin, either loyal or 'Communist' art on the one hand or 'Degenerate', 'Western', 'Anti-social' or 'Non-democratic' art on the other. Can doctrinaire prejudice plunge to more abysmal depths of absurdity than this?

Communism has been in power in Russia for over thirty-one years, so a Soviet citizen must be at least forty-five years of age to retain any clear recollection of conditions as they were in Tsarist days. This means that only the middle-aged and elderly can speak with any authority of conditions as they used to be in the 'old days' and, as a rule, these older people dare not speak their minds for fear of being denounced as reactionaries by the fanatical younger generation. In any case, of course, the percentage of those who can remember is growing less every year.

There seems little doubt that the Communist policy of deliberately breaking up the ties of family is adopted partly with the object of preventing the younger generations from being 'contaminated' (as they call it) with the old-fashioned ideas of the elders. The cleavage between these two sections of Russians is most marked, and is one of the most outstanding features to be noticed by any foreigner who gets, as I did, an opportunity of talking to the ordinary peasants of more remote villages. The old pre-revolutionary Russia is still very much alive among the older people, but it is as much as their lives are worth to air their feelings in front of youngsters, or anyone who might perhaps be a police spy of the M.V.D.

I will have more to write about the attitude of the elders when treating of religion in a later chapter.

The general result of all this is that the younger, and annually increasing, part of the population is being hermetically isolated from any sources of information which might give them an inkling of the outer world. They have nothing with which they can compare their present conditions—i.e. nothing except the fantastically perverted pictures of Western civilization which are concocted for their edification by the Kremlin. All books of pre-revolutionary Russian authors are kept away from them except those which paint Tsarist society and institutions in the blackest hue. The Lenin Library, which is a magnificent building, no doubt possesses copies of all these older books, but these are kept within an inner and closely guarded sanctum, only to be used as works of reference by high officials of the propaganda department. The elaborate system of checks and counter-checks in force at this great library is in itself an eye-opener as to the Soviet attitude toward free acquisition of knowledge by the people. In most Western countries we have our free libraries, where anyone can browse freely without being questioned as to his motives. At the Lenin Library knowledge and truth are locked away behind bars, and only released in small quantities at a time to those who can be trusted to pervert them for the good of the state.

Propaganda boasts are sometimes made by the Kremlin that Russians are free to listen to any foreign broadcast that they may fancy. This open-hearted attitude is often contrasted with that of the Nazis, who made it a criminal offence to listen to foreign broadcasts, or even in some cases to possess a listening set at all. Theoretically and 'on paper' this freedom of radio may exist. In actual practice it means nothing at all, because the vast masses of Soviet citizens are too desperately poor to be likely ever to own a wireless set of their own. In any case the complete lack of privacy in almost all the so-called 'homes' of the people would in practice make it impossible (and extremely unwise even if it were possible) to attempt to tune-in to any foreign station. Even if the would-be listener managed to tune-in to the foreign wave-length through the clamour of several other families around him, he would assuredly be reported sooner or later as one having Western sympathies; both he and his radio set would quickly disappear.

Though I had a wireless set in my own quiet flat, it was extremely difficult, even under those favourable conditions, to hear the B.B.C., chiefly owing to the continual blaring of local stations on practically the same wave-lengths. So boasts by Communists concerning the 'broadminded attitude' of the Soviet toward foreign broadcasts should be taken with a big pinch of salt.

The constant booming of official broadcasts by loud-speakers in public squares and parks is one of the 'amenities' of Soviet civilization to which the foreigner has to accustom himself.

Long established habits of juggling with the truth have produced in the mentality of Soviet officialdom an extraordinary attitude toward lying. They frequently put out a lie which is so blatant a lie that even they themselves cannot for one moment believe that anybody is going to swallow it. An example of this was the closing of the twelve motor roads 'for repairs', which I have recounted in Chapter II. It must have been obvious to the policemen on the spot, and to the authorities who put them there, that this story of 'repairs' would not deceive a baby, since a continual flow of Russian traffic was passing all the time. Normal people might have thought, 'Why bother to lie at all under these circumstances? It is simpler and more dignified to tell the truth and make no bones about it.' Not so the Soviet official. His mind appears to have lost all sense of difference between truth and falsehood as abstract commodities to be produced by the human tongue. He seems to act on the principle of telling a lie (in preference to the truth) and sticking to it, even when its absurdity has become apparent to all concerned. A most fantastic example of the lengths to which this weakness can go will be found in the strange story of my adventure with the village mob and its official sequel. ('Some Personal Adventures', Chapter V.)

Another example of this Soviet attitude to the truth can be found in their original excuses for imposing the economic blockade of Berlin—the excuses of 'technical difficulties' on the roads, railways, and waterways leading from the Western Zones. They can hardly have supposed that these pretexts would be taken seriously by the outside world. Yet they seem to have considered them worth the ink and paper expended upon them.

To a Westerner the truth is the truth, and nothing can alter it. We can, and do, lie like anybody else, but in doing so we know in our own minds that the truth is unaltered, and is something other than what we are saying. It almost seems as if the official Soviet mind has lost that attitude toward truth. A very peculiar characteristic of Soviet judicial proceedings and propaganda campaigns such as that against the musical composers (see pages 57-58), is the enormous importance attached to obtaining a 'voluntary' confession of his guilt by the victim. Everybody who has lived in a police-run country knows perfectly well how such confessions are extracted. Everybody knows the true value of such a confession as a contribution to valid evidence. The authorities know perfectly well that they have absolute power over their victim, that they can do what they like with him without need of any evidence at all. Yet they sometimes spend weeks or months in screwing out of their victim a 'voluntary' confession, which can make no difference whatsoever to their own powers of execution, and which cannot be expected to influence in the slightest degree the judgement of informed public opinion. What comfort does the conscience of Soviet officialdom get from these ridiculous 'voluntary' confessions? It almost seems as though to the warped mind of Communism truth is not something unalterable, but something which *can be altered* to suit Communist policy, either by means of an official statement or by the thumb-screws of the M.V.D.

This astounding trait in Communist mentality is, I suggest, something which ought to be studied more deeply than it has been studied so far by the normal outside world. It explains quite a lot of the seemingly inexplicable difficulties which the rest of the world has experienced in its dealings with the Soviet Union. It explains how the belauded heroes of one generation of Communism (Trotsky, Zinoviev, etc.) can become black-hearted traitors in the eyes of the next. Communism, in spite of its bitter contempt of all religion, is itself a religion, but it is a religion whose 'truths' are constantly being altered at the behest of the all-powerful upper hierarchy of the Communist Party—i.e. the Polit-Buro, the 'Fourteen Men of the Kremlin'.

That is the position of 'Truth' in the Soviet Union today.

She is treated as a slave of the government in power, as something to be twisted at their will out of all recognition. They, through their printing presses and schools, have the power to present the 'truth' in any shape or form they like to their own people. Through their Iron Curtain of frontier barriers and customs offices they have power to prevent truth from creeping in from the outer world. Even their own soldiers, who may during their service abroad have seen something of Western civilization, must first spend some long time in Siberia or some other 'political re-education' district before being allowed to go to their own homes and families. Through the police and M.V.D., people who are obnoxious to the government can be made to disappear suddenly from their homes, or even from the midst of a crowded street, without a word of the truth ever being allowed to escape from the mouths of those who might happen to have been present.

With such a strangle-hold on truth within their own country, it is not surprising that the leaders of Communism begin to think that they can strangle truth in the outer world also. It is up to civilized humanity to see that they are thwarted in this aim.

CHAPTER V

SOME PERSONAL ADVENTURES

AFTER the rather high level of discussion in the last chapter the time may perhaps be ripe for presenting, in the form of light relief, brief accounts of three experiences which befell me personally during my wanderings. They may be of interest as a means of giving, by concrete example, some picture of the state of affairs in that rather abnormal country.

Visit to a Concentration Camp

In using the word 'visit' I do not wish to give readers any impression that I was taken as an invited visitor to this sombre place. I must emphasize once more that never, during the whole of my stay in Russia, was I invited officially to visit *anything at all*, even of the mildest and least secret character, except cocktail parties and big ceremonial parades. The 'visit' which I am about to describe was entirely unintentional on my part, and emphatically not, I am afraid, in accordance with the wishes of the authorities. Even for a great reward I would not willingly repeat the experience.

It happened quite early in my time in Moscow. I was out walking one day, well distant from the capital, and was making a triangular course by compass through some wooded country with the intention of striking the same railway by which I had come out from Moscow, and then following it to the next station. I had no map, but it was fairly easy to navigate by compass, as the country was flat and without serious obstacles.

On coming to a piece of forest rather too dense to walk straight through, I noticed a grass-covered but dry watercourse which seemed to run approximately in the direction required. I descended into this little valley and followed it for about two miles. It took me right through the forest, roughly maintaining its original direction, though there were many curves and quite a large number of tributary ravines from both sides. The ravine was too deep to enable me to see anything on its banks except the tops of trees.

After about two miles these tree-tops thinned out, and I seemed to have reached more open ground. I came to a place where the ravine made a right-angled bend, which would have taken me off my course. Several minor valleys joined at this point, and it seemed an opportune moment to scramble back on to the higher ground to take my bearings and decide which of these subsidiary watercourses would serve my purpose best.

As I got near the top of the steep bank I heard voices, so I made in that direction with the intention of asking the way. Next moment I topped the rise and walked straight into something sinister and unpleasant.

On each of the promontories formed by all these ravines there was a hutted camp. Each camp was surrounded by a high double fence of barbed wire of unusually close mesh. Between the inner and outer fence in every case there was a flat space about twenty yards in width, without cover of any kind. The fences ran as far as possible in straight lines, and, wherever a bend was necessary, a wooden watch-tower stood at every corner. In each of these towers was standing a sentry of the M.V.D., armed with a tommy-gun.

There were many of these towers. I did not have time to see how many, nor did it seem wise to take that amount of interest in them. They were, on the average, not more than about a hundred yards apart. The voices which I had heard must have been the sentries, shouting to one another. The nearest tower was only a few yards from me, and its occupant was already eyeing me with puzzled suspicion.

What was the correct action to take? When I recounted this episode later to a friend in Scotland, a level-headed man but one who knew nothing of modern Russia, he was inclined to belittle the whole affair. His attitude was ,'Why not just explain who you were and apologize for the unintentional intrusion, and then withdraw?'

This nonchalant attitude of my friend was, I think, one of the first things that brought home to me forcibly the mental gulf which separates the two sides of the 'Iron Curtain', and the great difficulty in producing, for the edification of those who have not lived in a police-ridden state, the mental atmosphere which prevails in such places. In all probability, if I had been in Russia for only a few days, I might have acted just as my Scottish friend has suggested. Heaven knows what the result would have been. I *might* have been allowed to go in peace, but I very much doubt it. At any rate I had been just long enough in the country to know that the M.V.D. cannot be treated in the same friendly and confidential manner in which one would approach a London policeman. Instinctively I already had that feeling, common to almost everyone in the U.S.S.R., that the M.V.D. are people to be given as wide a berth as possible. Their distinctive head-dress, a forage cap with a red band and a top of very startlingly bright blue, has probably been chosen deliberately to make them conspicuous, and so to spread the terror of their presence among all Soviet citizens. There is no doubt whatever that it has this effect. Even to a foreigner on a peaceful country walk, and enjoying so-called 'diplomatic immunity', the sight of their red-and-blue caps and brutalized faces in this remote and obviously rather sinister place, sent an uncomfortable feeling down the spine.

Rightly or wrongly, at any rate, I did *not* walk up to the nearest sentry and tell him all about myself. In a flash I decided that the only thing to do was to walk on unconcernedly, as though I had every right to be there. Anything in the least bit out of the ordinary at once rouses the worst suspicions of the Russian petty official or sentry. Though my presence there was perfectly innocent, the very least that would have happened to me would have been hours and hours of delay, while somebody rang up someone else to find out if I might be allowed to proceed. Above all the very worst thing to do would have been to seem in any way lost, or hesitant, or guilty. So I walked straight on along the barbed wire fence, right past the sentry in his tower.

As I went, my eyes searched ahead anxiously for the best way out of this peculiar place. A few hundred yards ahead I saw a large number of people busily engaged in making what seemed to be either a new road or a new railway line. 'Good', I thought. 'That must be the way back to civilization. I will get on to that road and follow it, and so keep out of mischief.' So I strolled on as outwardly unconcerned as possible toward the large group of workers. It was not till I had got too close to them to turn back that I realized what sort of 'workers' they were.

There were, I should say, over three hundred of them, men and women, all dressed in the most filthy old rags. It was hard to guess their ages, for they all looked worn, weather-beaten, and nearly at the end of their days. Their complexions were grey, and the skin on their faces was like semi-transparent parchment. They were working stolidly, with their eyes turned toward the ground. They did not look frightened, or merely tired and half-starved, but something far surpassing these ordinary degrees of misery. They looked like people whose spirits had already died, but whose bodies kept on working mechanically. Their movements were slow and lethargic like those of half-wound clockwork toys. A few of the more robust ones had chains on their ankles, but for most of them the presence of still more M.V.D. guards among them, with rifles and fixed bayonets, seemed adequate safeguard against any risk of a dash for liberty. These M.V.D. men eyed me sourly and askance, but said nothing.

I walked right through the throng and continued down the track which they were making. A little further on it was flanked by more wooden huts, which seemed deserted. Thankfully I passed between the huts, still following the road, and emerged beyond them, but here a final shock awaited me. There was a road barrier across the track, and alongside it a sentry and his box. There was nothing for it now but to go straight ahead and hope for the best.

The barrier consisted merely of the usual pivoted pole to stop motor traffic. I walked up to it at what I fervently hoped would seem a natural pace, nodded curtly to the sentry, and ducked my head under the pole. I did not dare to look at the sentry again till I had gone another twenty or thirty yards. Then I cast a quick glance over my shoulder. He was standing gazing after me as though making up his mind what to do.

To my intense relief and joy the road ran straight ahead now, and apparently free of further obstacles. A few hundred yards on it re-entered the woods, and I could see the ravine, which I had left on the other side of the camp, now continuing its course parallel and close to the road. It seemed an age before I reached the edge of the woods and was lost to view from the camp. When I knew that I was safely out of sight, I left the road and descended into the friendly ravine, for I did not want to risk any further encounters with other working parties and their guards or any road traffic connected with that horrible place. After another two or three miles the ravine emerged among some open potato fields, so I left it and struck off across the plain and eventually found the railway again.

My Scottish friend made another illuminating remark when I told him this story. He asked, 'Who were these prisoners and what were they doing there?' He seemed surprised that I had not asked the guards for this information! It is possible, I suppose, that one might, in a normal country, indulge personal curiosity to this extent, though

I do not visualize myself asking such questions of (say) the warders on Dartmoor. But the very idea of anybody in Russia exhibiting such inquisitiveness to the M.V.D. is so fantastic as to emphasize still more the difference in outlook between those who have sensed the atmosphere of Russia and those who have not.

It was many days before I recovered sufficiently from the unpleasant recollection of this encounter to take any further walks in the country. When I did start them again, it can be well imagined that I was particularly careful in future not to stray from public roads or footpaths.

The Tale of an Old Sheepskin Coat

This episode, which earned for me a brief and entirely unnecessary publicity in the press of the world, was the first attempt of the authorities to intimidate me (and any other foreigners of similar recreational tastes) from wandering off the beaten track and seeing too much of social conditions behind the scenes. The absurdity of M.V.D. tactics is enhanced by the fact that on this particular occasion, far from being engaged in a walk through some remote country district, I was on a public thoroughfare in one of the suburbs of Moscow! Ever since the unpleasant affair of the concentration camp, I had been rather too deeply impressed by that experience to venture far afield again. On the particular occasion now to be described, I had just walked through the 'Gorki Park of Culture and Rest', one of the most public and open places in Moscow, and had just crossed the river by the public foot-bridge. The alleged 'photography', which formed the basis of this concocted incident, was said by the Russians to have taken place on this public footpath, and within full view of the sentry guarding the bridge over the river. It was hardly a likely place for clandestine photography!

After crossing the bridge I paused for a moment to look at the Lenin Hills, because I had been told that they were quite a good place for ski-ing. The public footpath here ran along the top of a railway embankment. There were crowds of other people walking along it and there was considerable traffic, mainly also pedestrian, on the roads just under the embankment. It was, in fact, about as public a place as could be found in one of Moscow's most public and ordinary suburbs. To the west of the embankment the river made a big loop along the foot of the Lenin Hills. In the loop of the river there was the usual untidy area of wood piles and semi-derelict buildings which were typical of the suburbs as a whole.

I had hardly started walking on again when a man stopped me and asked who I was and where I was going. The man's general demeanour was abrupt and offensive, so I enquired by what legal authority he spoke. He showed me some sort of a badge in the form of a large red star, which I accepted as being a genuine mark of officialdom. I therefore produced my identity card, whereupon the man snatched it from my hand and made off.

As it is both illegal and unsafe to go about Moscow without identity papers, I hurried after him, demanding the return of my card. He entered a small office and grabbed a telephone, at the same time signalling me to take a seat. Not knowing what was going on, I sat down

72

and listened to his talk on the telephone, which was to the effect that 'I have got him here. Please come along here quickly'. Having finished telephoning he turned very politely to me and said that someone wanted to speak to me. Would I kindly wait a moment?

A few minutes later in came a lieutenant-colonel of the railway service. He started in the blustering manner which seems typical of minor Soviet officials. Marching up to me he shouted:

'Where is your camera? Give it up to me.'

It seemed necessary to take this jack-in-office down a peg or two, so I asked him whether his companion, the plain-clothes man, had told him who I was, and whether that was the way in which Russian officers were taught to address senior officers of a foreign army that had recently fought as an ally of the U.S.S.R. This had the desired effect. He had the grace to apologize, and continued in a polite and respectful tone.

He then explained that someone had just reported having seen me taking photographs of a factory. I was still ignorant of the wiles of Soviet officialdom, so my immediate reaction was to assume that some foolish mistake had been made.

'That is easily disproved,' I told him. 'Please search me at once to see if I have got a camera.' But the plotters had already thought of this simple answer, and were prepared for it.

'Oh no,' he replied at once. 'We cannot do that. You see, you have a diplomatic pass, and diplomats are immune from search.'

73

'Very well,' said I. 'If diplomats are people entitled to so much respect, they must also be people whose word can be trusted. Either you take my word that I have no camera, or you may search me here and now. You cannot have it both ways.'

But Soviet officials are people who like to have it both ways. He still refused, and instead invited me to step across the road to the office of the factory, whose photograph I was said to have taken, in order to have a word with the director.

Still believing this to be merely a stupid mistake, and hoping that the director might prove to be a man of more common-sense than this uneducated officer, I accompanied him to the factory, which turned out to be the untidy group of semi-derelict buildings to which I have referred earlier. In the director's office we found the director himself, a youngish man with the air of a 'party member', and about ten other men sitting round the walls. The director greeted me politely enough and explained that all these men were the witnesses, who had seen the act of photography taking place. He invited me to take a chair and listen to their statements.

Once again I pointed out that it was quite unnecessary to waste time in that way, because I was perfectly willing to waive any diplomatic immunity and would agree then and there to be searched in order to settle the matter. But the director knew the right answer to that too. Producing a long piece of paper which he called an 'Act' he proceeded to read out a series of statements alleged to have been made by each of the men present. At the end of each statement he referred to one of these men for verification of the fact that this was his statement.

By now a strong suspicion was beginning to dawn upon me that this was no mere stupidity, born of the prevalent suspicion and spy-mania of Soviet petty officialdom, but a deliberately pre-arranged trick. The telephone conversation of the first man who had stopped me and his remark, 'I have got *him* here', and the readiness with which both lieutenant-colonel and factory-director had parried my offer to be searched—these things had already begun to arouse my suspicions. The production of this written 'act' by the director now confirmed my suspicions. There would have been no time for all these people to give their evidence to the director, *and have it all written down*, between the time I had halted for a moment on the embankment and my arrival in the director's office. Besides, what would have been the point in taking down all the evidence in writing before my arrival? The natural procedure would surely have been to wait till I arrived, so that I could be given an opportunity of hearing each witness giving his own testimony. I realized that something deep and dirty was afoot.

Accordingly I interrupted the director, after he had read a couple of these 'statements', to point out to him that, although I had a fair knowledge of Russian, it was not in keeping with normal standards of equity to conduct what was now amounting to a serious accusation against some person in a language which that person could only partially understand. I demanded that before we proceeded any further, an interpreter should be summoned. I also

75

demanded that a telephone call should be put through either to the British Embassy or to General Seraev's office. None of these requests was granted, the excuse in each case being the favourite Soviet pretext of 'technical difficulties'. Telephonic communication with the centre of Moscow had suddenly become unaccountably bad, and they regretted that there was nobody in reach who spoke any English at all.

When the director had finished the solemn farce of reading the 'statements' to the 'witnesses' and asking each in turn if he agreed with the evidence, he passed the 'act' over to me and invited me to sign it! I could scarcely credit the naïve effrontery of the man. Naturally I refused to do anything of the kind.

The director seemed genuinely surprised at this, and for some time continued to try to persuade me that it was 'merely a matter of form', which would not in any way imply my admission of any part of the statement. When he finally realized that I was not fool enough to be taken in, he suddenly stood up and handed me back my identity card.

'Then there is no more to be said. Good day.'

But now it was my turn. I pointed out to him that much of my time had been wasted without any justification. I did not now intend to leave his office till he had got a telephone call through to General Seraev's office. I intended to wait there till General Seraev himself or one of his staff officers came there with a car to take me back to my flat.

The director probably began now to wish that he had got a telephone call through when my request was first made, for it was about an hour and a half more before a staff officer and a car could be summoned. During this time I sat in his office, and must considerably have dislocated and delayed the normal work of the office. At last Captain Pasko, a naval officer on General Seraev's staff, arrived in a car.

For the third time I made the request that Captain Pasko, as one authorized to deal with foreign attachés, should search me in order to disprove the existence of a camera. He made the same reply as the other two. I then demanded that he should drive me straight to General Seraev so that I could explain the matter to him and prove to his satisfaction that the whole story was without foundation. Pasko agreed to this, but, no sooner were we on the way in the car than he told me that General Seraev was out of Moscow, and could not therefore be visited that evening.

Such was the affair as it actually occurred. I will now give readers a close translation of the account of this same incident, as it appeared in *Pravda* on the following Monday in the form of a letter to the Editor, purporting to have been sent by 'four factory workers'. It should be remembered by all who do not know Russia that nobody in that country seriously believes for one moment that any letter to the Editor is ever written by 'four factory workers' or any other private individuals, but invariably by the propaganda organization of the government. This is what the letter said:

'Dear Editor,

'The occurrence we wish to write about has caused deep

77

indignation among the workers at our factory and *deserves to be brought to the notice of the Soviet general public.*

'On October 30th, at midday, a stranger in a *well-worn and tattered sheepskin jacket and worker's boots* was noticed on a railway bridge not far from our factory. He was facing the factory and taking photographs. The appearance of the stranger *naturally* attracted the attention of the workers, and they immediately informed members of the factory guard. When he observed the factory guard approaching the stranger hastily left the bridge and began to make off hurriedly. He was overtaken. ...

'The stranger *in the tattered sheepskin jacket* produced the identity card of a diplomat and called himself the British Military Attaché in Moscow, Major-General Hilton. ...

'A member of the Department for External Relations was summoned to the factory, and he established beyond all doubt that the person *in the well-worn and tattered sheepskin coat* was in fact ... General Hilton.

'... He tried to deny the fact that he had with him a camera and that he was photographing the factory. His presence near the factory he tried to explain by saying that he was looking for a place for ski-ing.

'Frankly this explanation seemed unconvincing to our workers. One cannot understand what need there is for a British general, who suddenly takes it into his head to busy himself with such a pressing matter as looking for a place for ski-ing, *to dress himself up in a tattered sheepskin coat.*

'Our workers see this incident differently. *Are not certain foreign diplomats*, in their activity in Moscow, attempting to use the same means as their colleagues in the Balkans? (etc., etc.).'

There was some more padding, which I have cut for brevity. The italics were not in the original, but are my own, because I wish to draw attention to them. The first paragraph (reference to the 'Soviet general public') and the last (reference to the activities of 'foreign diplomats') give the clue to the *raison-d'être* of the whole affair. It was intended to show the Soviet people what sinister villains all we foreigners are. The word 'naturally' is worth notice in passing. If the affair had really been natural and un-premeditated, it would surely have been more 'natural' for the factory guards themselves to notice the mysterious stranger, rather than have to get a report about him from the 'workers' who, one would presume, would have been hard at work. Far from being 'natural', the true explana-tion is much more likely to be that initiation of the plot had to be entrusted to reliable 'party' men who happened to be workers and not mere factory guards.

It is worth noting also that no mention is made of the military sentry on the bridge, in front of whose nose the alleged 'photography' took place. Nor is any mention made of the locality. These two details would have spoiled the story from a propaganda point of view in the eyes of all who knew that very harmless and public suburb of Moscow. Nor is there any mention of my offer to be searched.

But the real cream of the letter lies in its repeated reference to 'the tattered sheepskin coat'. The object of inserting this item, and of the emphasis placed upon it, is of course quite obviously to convey the impression that the mysterious stranger was creeping about heavily disguised (though why he should be so foolish as to select the top of a railway bridge for his conspicuous act of villainy the writers of the letter discreetly left unexplained).

Mention of the 'tattered sheepskin coat' was almost a masterpiece of propaganda, but unfortunately for its authors, it gave us the final proof that the whole thing had been worked out deliberately. I need hardly say that I most certainly was not wearing such a garment on this particular occasion. Even in a city of such badly-dressed people as Moscow, I am not quite eccentric enough to walk about the suburbs in rough country clothes. But it did so happen that I *possessed* an old sheepskin coat, which I intended to wear later on in the winter for ski-ing expeditions out in the country. On this particular day it was hanging safely in my wardrobe at the flat. How then did the 'four factory workers' know that I possessed such a garment other than through someone (the propaganda experts) supplying them with this information and instructing them to use it as a piquant bit of 'local colour'? Knowing that my domestic staff (poor wretches) were forced to give the M.V.D. the fullest possible reports on all my private affairs, it could be assumed as a certainty that the authorities knew of the existence of this old coat. What more natural than the temptation to embroider their story by dragging in the old coat, knowing that I could not deny possession of some such old garment?

It was unfortunate for them that they did so, because this over-doing of the 'local colour' gave their whole game away. As time went by, and it became obvious to the entire diplomatic community that the Kremlin did not intend to follow the matter up by demanding my removal from Russia, the absurdity of the whole affair became obvious. It was not likely that the government would countenance the continued residence in Moscow of a foreign attaché whom they genuinely believed to have been guilty of espionage. The fact that the Kremlin made no effort to have me recalled, and that I was finally withdrawn at my own request more than seven months later, seems to indicate that they did not really believe their own official story.

Whatever the trick may have been intended to achieve, it fizzled out after a few weeks like a damp squib. There was the usual unsatisfactory exchange of diplomatic notes. Quite a lot of cheap fun was extracted at my expense by newspaper cartoonists and by the chief comedian, Karand'ash, of the Moscow Circus, who staged a very witty and amusing act with a pair of skis and a camera. It was all good clean fun; and for my own part I was only too delighted to give the people of Moscow something to laugh about. They certainly need it.

The affair also provided the organizers of Moscow's great 'spontaneous demonstrations of loyalty' with one extra subject for their wit and ingenuity. It is customary after a great ceremonial military parade on the Red Square for thousands of civilian 'volunteers' (rather the sergeant-major's kind of volunteers) to file past the Polit-Buro on top of Lenin's Tomb, accompanied by decorated lorries representing topical events or pillorying notorious foreigners. On one of these occasions I enjoyed the high distinction of figuring by proxy in one of these cars, complete with skis, camera, and 'old sheepskin coat', in company with no less distinguished victims than Mr Winston Churchill and President Truman! This was fame indeed!

Within a couple of weeks of this absurd affair it had already become obvious that, whatever the object of the Soviet authorities may have been, it had failed. Its propaganda value among their own people seems to have been negligible. I found the ordinary non-official classes if anything more friendly to me than before. Had they believed that there was any truth at all in the espionage implication they would certainly not have been friendly, for the poorest Russians, in spite of all that they have to suffer, are still intensely patriotic. There is little doubt that, in spite of all the cartoons and propaganda built upon this case in the governmental press, the ordinary people did not believe a word of it. A short while after the publication of the 'four factory workers'' letter, I met an old peasant couple, with whom I had chatted very amicably once or twice on my previous country walks. Rather sadly I imagined that they would now no longer want to have any more to do with me and said so to them. But the old woman, after first looking about carefully to see that nobody but her husband was listening, said, 'We have both lived in this country long enough to know the real value of *Pravda*.' Whether she was referring to the newspaper or to the lady who lives in the bottom of a well I was not quite certain, but it was clear enough what she thought of the fantastic tale of the 'four factory workers'.

As to the second probable motive of the authorities in concocting this incident—i.e. the intimidation of myself and any other foreigners from taking country walks— through their stupidity in choosing this particular locality for their trick it had exactly the opposite effect to that which they must have intended. For my own part I came to the conclusion that, if this sort of trick was liable to be played upon me even when walking in the suburbs of Moscow, I might just as well resume my country walks further afield. Ever since the unpleasant affair of the concentration camp I had refrained from distant country walks, and had restricted myself to the suburbs. Now I realized that if the authorities wished to be nasty they would be so wherever I took my walks, so I might as well take to the country again.

Though this affair, which created a mild stir in Moscow for a day or two after publication of the 'factory workers' ' letter, very quickly fizzled out locally, its repercussions abroad, thanks to the love of sensationalism in some of our own papers, were out of all proportion to the actual importance of the case, and led to the making of some extremely misinformed and stupid remarks by people who ought to have had more sense. Thus, for example, Mr Emrys Hughes, M.P., remarked in Parliament: 'In view of the unfortunate incident which occurred in Moscow, will my Hon. Friend (the Secretary of State for Foreign Affairs) consider withdrawing him (i.e. the military attaché) and sending to Moscow somebody who would be more likely to bring understanding with the Soviet Union?' The reply given to this M.P. was, 'No, sir. I entirely reject the suggestion that our Military Attaché was in any way at fault in the incident.'

Perhaps Mr Emrys Hughes has never been taught the wisdom and ordinary decency of hearing both sides of a matter before airing his views about it. Perhaps he also realizes by now that other people besides the writer of this book have found some difficulties in reaching 'understanding with the Soviet Union'. Stupidities of this kind, perpetrated by people who hardly know the first thing about the Soviet Union and its ways, must have consoled the instigators of this affair considerably for their almost complete failure within the U.S.S.R.

The Adventure in Perlovka Woods

Three weeks after the affair of the 'old sheepskin coat' the Soviet authorities struck their next blow. This time again the plot misfired through clumsy handling by the people on the spot, but the actual results were quite unpleasant enough for me.

This time I was walking through some woods to the immediate north-east of Moscow. I have given their name so that any reader who may happen to know Moscow will more clearly be able to realize the harmlessness of my choice of route. These woods bear roughly the same relation to Moscow that Richmond Park or Wimbledon Common bears toward London. The Perlovka Woods were in summer time a favourite locality for picnics among the diplomatic community. Even at the height of their campaign against the freedom of movement of foreigners, never before had the authorities shown the slightest objection to foreigners visiting these woods and roaming about them. Londoners who read this will be able to get some idea of the sort of country that Russia is today if they visualize some harmless foreigner on a Sunday walk through Richmond Park undergoing the adventure which I will now recount.

It was Sunday the 23rd November. There was deep snow in the woods, which made the going very difficult except on a few well-beaten paths. This suited my purpose, for I had now adopted the rule of never going anywhere off roads or footpaths that were in full use by the public. In this way I hoped to avoid blundering again into anything (such as the concentration camp) which foreign eyes were not intended to see. The snow made it quite easy for me to see which of the forest paths were in frequent and regular use. There were many people in the wood collecting timber, and their hand-drawn sledges had flattened and hardened the snow on a good many paths and made them quite easy for walking. It was bitterly cold, so I stepped along at a fast pace, and after a couple of hours I sat down on a stump to eat my sandwiches. I was still on a well-worn path, but for the moment there were no wood-gatherers near me.

Soon after starting again the track rounded a little bend and I saw four men standing in the path. They did not move aside as I approached, so I had to step off the path into the deeper snow to get past them. The men viewed me intently, but said nothing till I had gone a few yards past them. One of them then hailed me, and enquired whether I was a Russian. On my replying that I was English the spokesman, a tall man who seemed to be some kind of a game-keeper or head forester, asked to see my identity card, which I showed. This time, however, remembering the trick played upon me three weeks ago, I did not let go of my card.

The four men appeared to be quite satisfied, and merely asked whence I had come and whither I was going. I made a point of asking them whether there was any objection to my presence in the wood, and whether the track upon which we were standing was open to the public or not. They assured me that all was in order and let me proceed.

Ten minutes or so later I reached a track junction where (according to my compass) I ought to have turned right in order to get back to Perlovka, the village from which I had started my walk, and where my car was awaiting me. Both the path to the right and that which ran straight ahead were well used by the public. As I turned to the right there was a shout behind me. Looking round, I saw the tall forester following me at a distance of about a hundred yards. He shouted, 'No. Straight on'.

At this stage of proceedings I had no reason to suspect that he had any other object in view except to guide me on my way. It was possible that the right-hand track, though seeming to be my correct direction, might merely be a blind alley. I took his advice and walked on. He continued to follow me.

86

Soon after this we came to a clearing, and ahead of us I could see, about a mile away across some fields, a village, and beyond it was a main road with motor traffic passing at frequent intervals. The broad well-worn path ran straight on to this village, but there was a little narrow path, on which the snow still lay deep and undisturbed, which branched off at this point and led back into the woods. About a quarter of a mile distant in the direction taken by this little path I could see the roofs of a group of buildings.

As soon as the forester saw that I had passed this little turning, and was continuing on the broad track, he began shouting to me to take the little path into the woods. I looked along it doubtfully and hesitated, for it certainly did not look like a public footpath. Indeed I was almost sure that I could see part of a high wire fence and a wooden watch-tower. Seeing my hesitation the forester at once became furiously angry, and blustered almost incoherently, pointing again and again down the little path.

By this time I was beginning to 'smell a rat', so I thanked him politely for showing me the way so far, and told him that I could now dispense with his company. At this he became still more excited and abusive, and refused to go away. I was getting a little bored with him by now, so I sat down on a heap of snow and waited for him to go.

This puzzled him for a moment. His flow of language abated and he looked at me curiously. Then he came close to me and lowered his voice to a confidential whisper.

'Give me one hundred roubles,' he said. 'Then I will go.'

87

'Why the hell should I give you money?' I retorted. 'To start with I have not got a hundred roubles on me.' 'Yes you have,' he replied. 'I saw it.'

Then I realized that, when I had pulled my identity card out of my wallet, the edges of a few notes must have protruded from the wallet. 'Give me a hundred roubles,' he repeated. 'Then I will go away. If not, then I make trouble. I call the police.'

I ignored this and sat on calmly. After waiting a while he suddenly lost his temper again and shook his fist in my face and then lifted his foot as though to kick me.

I felt that it was time to take a firm line with him, so I jumped up and told him very forcibly that I intended to walk across the fields to the village. He got into my way and waved his left fist at me, fumbling for something in his pocket with the right hand. It seemed as though a fight was inevitable, so I squared up to him with my fists, but at the last moment he thought better of it and stepped out of my way, growling furiously.

During all this time I still thought that I had only to deal with a blackmailer or robber, working for his own ends. It seemed, therefore, that the best thing that I could do would be to get to the village and the main road. I walked briskly across the fields and the forester followed, shouting and cursing. It began to dawn upon me that the man must be something more than a mere footpad.

At the entrance of the village there were two soldiers, mending telegraph wires. There were also many peasants clearing snow off the village street. When we got close to the soldiers the forester pulled a police whistle out of his pocket and blew it several times, and then began shouting again.

The soldiers stopped their work and looked towards us for a moment. Then they rushed at me, waving and shouting. Several men and youths also broke away from the crowd in the village and ran towards me. In a moment I was surrounded by an angry mob, punching me in the face, kicking me on the shins, and apparently trying to drag my clothes off me. The din was chaotic. Everybody was shouting advice or threats at the top of his voice. The two soldiers took charge of proceedings and began to drag me along towards the village. In vain I tried to ask them what it was all about. The tumult was so great that I could hardly hear my own voice. Then one of the soldiers yelled into my ear:

'Where is your weapon?'

'I have no weapon,' I shouted back at him.

'Yes you have. *He* says so (pointing at the forester). He says that you attacked him.'

It was in vain that I tried to assure the crowd that I had no weapon. They were in no mood to listen. When we reached the first house of the village, the crowd began to drag me up an out-door staircase, leading to a loft. I had hoped till now that we were going to a police station, but this dark and dingy building was obviously nothing of the kind. I started to remonstrate again and tried to argue with the crowd, but this only made them more violent.

Up the stairs we went, and into a dark loft, where many hands at once proceeded to search me from head to foot.

89

There was no nonsense this time about diplomatic immunity from search! Of course they found no weapon. Fortunately I had not even a penknife on me. At this the crowd calmed down considerably, and began to look a little worried at what they had done. One of the soldiers said, rather sheepishly:

'But he told us that you attacked him with a weapon. Where is it?'

'Yes. Where is it?' I taunted him. 'You had better have another look. There will be very serious trouble over this. Which one of us two is the liar—this man or I?' The crowd now began to show some hostility to the tall forester, but not for long. A quick sign passed between him and the soldiers. (The 'sleuths' of the M.V.D. have got some method of establishing their identity. I met it once again in a case which I have already mentioned, when my assistant and I gave a couple of 'sleuths' in charge for loitering after us with felonious intent. In both cases it was done much too quickly for me to see what happened.)

The attitude of the two soldiers changed, and they began to bluster and threaten me. It was time, I decided, that this affair should get into more responsible hands, so I demanded to be taken to the nearest police station. After a vociferous argument between the soldiers and the forester, in which the crowd joined, it was at last decided that it would be better to hand the whole affair over to the police. The forester, I could clearly see, was in a most awkward quandary. Something had obviously gone wrong with his plans, and in Russia the penalty for failure is very severe indeed. I do not, of course, know to this day what those plans were, but it was clear that everything depended upon inveigling me down that little path toward the rather sinister-looking buildings. Perhaps it also depended on 'framing' me with a faked charge of attempted bribery, if I had been foolish enough to give him any money. I can only suppose that the forester, who was certainly a man of ungovernable temper, lost his head when he saw that 'plans' were misfiring, and in his rage he blurted out this story of an attack so as to incite the mob against me.

During the long and angry argument which now surged around me, he took the line that 'the less said the better" but the two soldiers and the crowd thought otherwise. They knew that they had put themselves very seriously in the wrong, and that the consequences might be serious, so they were all in favour of reporting the affair to the police at once and making it clear that they had acted on the story of this M.V.D. 'sleuth'. What might happen to him they obviously did not care in the least as long as they could 'pass the baby'. I am quite sure that the 'forester' would dearly have liked to have me quietly murdered, so that no repercussions of this day's work should fall on him. Had there been fewer people present he might have arranged this, but now the presence of an entire village population was my safeguard. It was touch and go for a while, as the argument swung back and forward, but in the end the desire of the whole village to 'play for safety' prevailed. It was decided that we should all go to the police station in a village some distance away and report the whole affair to the authorities. The 'forester' made a gallant effort to slip quietly away, but one of the soldiers spotted him, and he was forced to accompany us. The behaviour of the soldiers toward me was now most correct. They made themselves responsible for the safe custody of my personal possessions, which had been taken from my pockets, and even clouted a village youth who was filching a rouble or two out of my wallet, and forced him to give back his ill-gotten gains.

The village bus was brought out and we all boarded it. In another twenty minutes or so we reached the police station. (I gathered that Goliyanovo, the village where the fracas occurred, possessed no police station of its own.) From now on the affair pursued the dreary and laborious procedure of Soviet police investigations. At every stage the 'forester' tried hard to convince his hearers that he had been acting under instructions and that they ought not to interfere, but the bluff did not come off.

It was obvious that this particular police station had not been 'briefed' about any plot against a foreigner. Therefore what had happened in their village of Goliyanovo (since it must have been within their jurisdiction) might have adverse repercussions on them unless they also 'played for safety'. Accordingly police officer after police officer 'passed the baby' to his next superior, till I began to think that I was not going to get home to my flat till the matter had been referred to the Kremlin itself.

The proceedings in the police station dawdled on for about three and a half hours. Finally a lieutenant-colonel of police arrived, a correct and reasonably courteous officer. He apologized for what had occurred, ascribing it to the 'ignorance of a mere peasant', and told me that he had sent for a car to take me home.

It was now long after dark. Presently the car arrived. In it were three plain-clothes men of rather sinister aspect. One of them drove, and the other two invited me to sit between them on the back seat. Unpleasant memories of gangster films, in which the victim was 'taken for a ride', surged into my head, and I began to wonder whether the 'forester' had succeeded in converting others to his solution of the problem. However, all was well. They returned me safe and sound to my flat in Moscow.

The sequel to this curious affair is perhaps the most amazing thing of all. It need hardly be mentioned that next day there was sent from our embassy an extremely strongly worded protest to the Soviet Ministry of Foreign Affairs. To this important and formal communication *no reply whatsoever was given for seven weeks*. At the end of this time, in response to many reminders and requests that the matter should receive attention, Mr Molotov himself penned a reply, the significant portion of which was the Kremlin's own version of this incident. I would like to leave it to the judgement of readers of normal intelligence in free countries to decide for themselves which of these two versions they prefer to believe, only pointing out that, if Mr Molotov himself really believed the story which emerged under his signature, it seems rather a remarkable thing that he did not demand my immediate departure from Russia. Surely an occurrence such as he describes would, within twenty-four hours of its happening, have been followed by a categorical demand for the immediate withdrawal of the perpetrator, if not a more severe action against him. Instead of which no action at all emanated from the Soviet authorities for seven weeks. Even then they were content to put forward this story and leave the alleged perpetrator in full possession of his diplomatic status in Moscow!

Here is the Soviet official version, as extracted from Mr Molotov's letter:

'As has been established by the investigation which has been made, on 23rd November, near a military aerodrome where the local inhabitants are not accustomed to walk, there appeared an unknown person in a short sheepskin coat and in a worn cloak!

'The watchman thought this unknown person to have a suspicious appearance, especially as he refused to produce evidence of his identity and attempted to hide himself. Moreover this unknown person threatened the watchman with a knife, as a result of which the watchman was compelled to appeal for help to two soldiers, who were close by, and who detained the unknown person. When one of the soldiers demanded that the knife should be handed over, the unknown person replied that he had thrown it away in the wood. When the unknown person was brought to Moscow City Militia, he produced a document in the name of General Hilton, Attaché of the British Embassy in Moscow, whereupon he was set free.'

Please take your choice, readers, as to which of these two stories you find the more credible. The ingenious explanation of the non-existence of any knife is particularly worthy of study. If the two soldiers were 'close by' when the watchman was threatened, this sinister 'unknown person' must have been a bit of a conjurer to have disposed of the knife so cleverly. It was rather stupid of him, surely, to have obligingly admitted that he had 'thrown it away in the wood'!

But the most astonishing feature of the affair, to my mind, is the fact that Mr Molotov himself, who signed this most serious accusation against me, shortly afterwards invited me to one of his receptions, and received me with courtesy and apparent friendliness. One would imagine that a dangerous and violent character like this 'unknown person' would be cut dead from all future hospitality of Soviet officialdom, even if, for some extraordinary reason, the Kremlin did not demand his instant withdrawal from the country. On the contrary, I continued to be invited to all official functions, and on the occasion of Red Army Day (20th February) my treatment at the hands of Marshal Vassilevsky and other marshals was most cordial and friendly. The ways of Soviet officialdom are indeed most unaccountable and odd!

Readers may wonder how this incident, and the previous case of alleged photography, could have been 'laid on' deliberately by the authorities, assuming my theory to be correct that they were, in fact, 'put-up jobs'. Such a thing is not nearly as difficult to arrange in the Soviet Union, where the M.V.D. is all-powerful, as it would be in a civilized country. I have already described the elaborate system of 'sleuthing' which was in force. In those early days I had not yet perfected my technique for getting rid of these obnoxious hangers-on, and it is quite probable that one or more may have been following me on these occasions. It would be quite easy for him, as soon as he saw which direction I was taking, to telephone ahead to some police post to make arrangements for something to be prepared against me, or, in the forest case, to get ahead of me while I halted for lunch.

Or, alternatively, it would have been a simple matter for the M.V.D. to circulate my photograph to plain-clothes men all over the suburbs and surrounding district, giving instructions that anyone recognizing me must start some sort of a case. This might have accounted for the clumsy tactics of the 'forester'.

CHAPTER VI

THE POWER OF THE M.V.D.

THIS incident of the 23rd November and its sequel seven weeks later gave me grounds for very serious thought. Bluntly it meant that *anything* could happen to a foreigner in this country without a word of the truth ever leaking out. In England, or any other civilized country, there was no power in the land that could silence the tongues of a whole village in the way that the people of Goliyanovo had been silenced. If a tumult took place in an English village, involving violent assault upon a foreigner, some trickle of gossip about the affair would almost certainly reach the ears of local journalists. It would be impossible to keep the matter dark. Between violent assault and murder there is only a difference of degree. If the 'forester' had won his point in the argument, and had persuaded the village to get rid of me, there is every reason to suppose that the powers who control 'truth' in Russia would have silenced the tongues of local gossips just as effectively as they actually did in this case.

The power of the M.V.D. is absolute. He who controls the M.V.D. controls Russia, subject, of course, to the fact that he in turn is controlled by the Polit-Buro as a whole, and is bound to act in accordance with the 'Party Line'— i.e. the policy decided by the Polit-Buro. Does Marshal Stalin control the Polit-Buro, or does he act merely as senior member and chairman? Nobody outside that select coterie is ever likely to know. But one thing at least is certain. The policy initiated by the Polit-Buro is the policy that rules the Soviet Union and everything that happens within its territory. No consideration of truth or of fair treatment of individuals is allowed to stand in the way of implementation of the accepted policy, laid down by this all-powerful body. The Minister of the Interior himself is one of the three or four most important members of this oligarchy, and the M.V.D. is his machine for carrying out the Polit-Buro's policy.

It is true that on paper the Soviet Union has got quite an elaborate constitutional government, consisting of a President, a Praesidium, a Supreme Soviet, a Soviet of Nationalities, and a system of 'elections'. I do not propose to study this constitution in detail for two reasons. Firstly full information regarding it is already available in print for those who may be interested, including the composition of the sixteen autonomous republics which compose the U.S.S.R. and the many semi-autonomous statelets contained within the R.S.F.R. (the essentially *Russian* portion of the whole Soviet Union). All this is extremely interesting to the theoretical student of governmental institutions, but its practical value at present is diluted by the undoubted fact that the U.S.S.R. is an oligarchy, ruled from the top by the fourteen or so chief men of the Communist Party; and it is ruled in the interests of that party and of no others. Little or no pretence is made that the so-called 'elections' are anything but an invitation to the people as a whole to come, like obedient 'yes-men', to endorse the activities of their masters the Communists by slavishly recording a vote for some nominee of the Party. As a Soviet citizen, you may vote for a Communist or not vote at all. In the latter case you may run considerable risk of incurring the name of being 'anti-social', which is dangerously near to becoming an 'enemy of the people'. So in practice most people do vote, but the lack of enthusiasm or interest evinced by the common people at election time, though understandable under the circumstances, is pathetic when compared to election-fever in any genuine democracy.

The Supreme Soviet meets once a year, and as far as one can see its principal duty is to put the seal of official approval on all that the government has done in the interval. The very chamber where they meet strongly suggests an assembly of 'yes-men' rather than a free parliament of deputies with the courage of their own opinions. It is situated in the main palace of the Kremlin The seating accommodation is arranged, not as in our own Parliament or in any other assembly where debate is the normal procedure, but in rows of seats all facing the same direction, like the desks of a schoolroom. In front of these rows of desks is a raised rostrum, where the real controllers of proceedings evidently take control. Behind the seats of the deputies there are some raised 'boxes', in which can sit observers who can scrutinize the deputies from behind their backs, and note down, if necessary, anybody who dares to take a firm and independent line on any matter.

The sight of this meeting place of the 'people's representatives', together with my observations round the streets of Moscow during the great day of the elections— these two things were, I am afraid, sufficient to cure me of any tendency to take the paper constitution very seriously. The only power that really matters in the Soviet Union is the power of the M.V.D., the instrument of the Communist Party, or more particularly of its executive committee, the Polit-Buro.

The meaning of the initials M.V.D. has already been explained. Strictly speaking it denotes the Ministry of the Interior itself (*Anglice* 'Home Office'), but in practice it has come to mean the 'Home Secretary's' own special army for keeping the country in order. The uniformed and armed portion of this *corps d'élite* is reputed to number over 600,000 men. This force is not organized as an ordinary police force or gendarmerie, but as a small and highly efficient army with its own complete divisions of all arms. These big formations would be quite capable of conducting large-scale mobile field operations against any community who might venture upon armed insurrection anywhere behind the Iron Curtain. These divisions could even, if ever it became necessary, take on the divisions of the Red Army itself. I do not suggest for a moment that this ever will become necessary. The hold which the Party exercises over the Red Army by more subtle means will probably be sufficient. But it is important to remember that the M.V.D. exists as 'an army behind the Army'—an army, moreover, of carefully picked men, whose loyalty to the régime has been checked and counter-checked till there can be no doubt about it, and whose training and general efficiency is about 50 per cent higher than that of the ordinary soldiers.

But it is the ubiquitous ramifications of the M.V.D.'s system of police-spies, *agents-provocateurs*, and informers, that make this force such a terror throughout the land and ensure it such an absolute hold upon everything that happens in the Soviet Union. I have written enough of the surveillance of foreigners, and of the unscrupulous campaign of intimidation and calumny which the M.V.D. can and does work up against any foreigner who dares to behave as though he is in a normal land.

Such treatment is not for the foreigners alone. Every Soviet citizen is spied upon continually by somebody. Even the spies themselves are spied upon by other spies, without either being aware of the other's identity or activities. This is not merely hearsay evidence or second-hand 'thriller stuff'. In my own personal experience I came upon many instances of this spying by Russians on Russians, and proofs of the abject terror which this nightmare kind of existence brings to harmless, helpless, and obscure people of the poorer non-official classes. I cannot, in fairness to these humble and innocent people, be explicit in giving detailed instances, because to do so might bring upon them the special attention of the dreaded M.V.D. I can only give my word of honour that I do personally know of many such cases, both during my time in Moscow and my previous year in the Soviet Zone of Germany. I personally have seen a man of fine physique and decent self-respecting character literally vomiting with fear because he thought that something perfectly harmless that he had done might be reported to the M.V.D. I have seen an old peasant couple reduced to shivering despair

101

because the husband had suddenly received a summons to report to the local M.V.D. office the coming night. They parted from one another as though he was off on some terribly dangerous enterprise from which he was unlikely ever to return. As things turned out all was well on this particular occasion, but the poor old couple went through several hours of agonized suspense before he went.

That is an important part of the technique of the M.V.D. —to reduce their victims to a state of abject terror before they even start to question them. Partly for this reason investigations are always carried out at night, and are continued into the small hours of the morning, so that the nerves of the victim, already strained by many hours of suspense the previous day, will become frayed and exhausted, and his tongue will thereby be loosened. It also has the advantage that the general population will not know the identity of all those who visit the M.V.D. report centre after dark.

In the Soviet Zone of Germany the work of the blue-and-red capped M.V.D. is performed by another force, the green capped 'frontier guards', but their methods are very similar. Next door to our headquarters in Potsdam there was a security report centre, the windows of which were a blaze of light to all hours of the night. Local Germans (except gangsters of the S.E.D.*) gave the place a very wide berth, and every artifice was employed by the green caps to give the place an air of ill-omen and terror.

Those who attend these nocturnal sessions fall into three

* S.E.D. = 'Sozialistiche Einheit Deutschland,' the Soviet-sponsored German political party.

classes. There are those who receive an occasional or special summons to attend, such as the old peasant man whom I have mentioned. This may happen to any Soviet citizen at any time. Then there are people who may be employed in any capacity as normal citizens, but who also have the additional job of reporting regularly to the M.V.D. How these people originally start being police-spies varies. In some cases this work is undertaken most unwillingly, and only under threat of dire reprisals upon the victim or upon relatives if reports are not forthcoming. But in this class also there are many wretches who voluntarily undertake the work as a spare-time job for the sake of extra rations. All this class, the 'regular' reporters, are fully briefed by the M.V.D. exactly as to what items they are to include in their reports. It is an understood thing that all Soviet citizens who are permitted by the authorities to work for any foreigner must undoubtedly belong to this class of reporters.

The third type are the most unpleasant and sinister of all. These are the professional police-spies and *agents-provocateurs*. In most cases they also have another job, but in their case that job is only a cover for their real activities. Amongst their duties is that of spying upon all the other spies who may be working in the same factory, workshop, or retail magazine. The essence of the game is that nobody should know who else besides himself or herself is employed in this dirty work.

It would be difficult to arrive at any estimate of the total numbers of men and women (and probably children also) employed as spies by the M.V.D. in the second and third of the categories mentioned above. There is firm reason to believe that the 'professionals' alone—i.e., the plain-clothes sleuths who pass themselves off as something else and who mix in every community down to the smallest village group—must run into several hundred thousand paid spies.

On top of all this it must be remembered that every boy or girl is taught from the first moment of joining the 'Pioneers' the sacred duty of 'healthy suspicion'—i.e. the duty of reporting and denouncing anything which may seem to the child to be worthy of notice by the M.V.D. Among a people never far removed from the starvation line, it is natural that this early teaching should breed a considerable number of wretches sufficiently lost to all sense of human decency to curry favour with the M.V.D. by creeping round to them with tales of their closest neighbours.

The fighting services themselves do not escape this nightmare of police-spying. Till recently the system in vogue was to appoint to every unit of the Army and every ship of the Navy a 'political officer' or commissar, with his own staff of N.C.O.s or petty officers of the same ilk as himself. He usually figured as second-in-command of the outfit, the commander himself being a straightforward fighting man. Though this system has now been officially abolished, it is probable that something on very similar lines is still in force. Again and again in my dealings with senior army officers I had unmistakable confirmation of the fact that the apparent commander was not really complete master in his own command, but that in some respects he had to take his orders from one of his own junior officers. One example of this will suffice.

During my year in the Soviet Zone of Germany we were once returning to Potsdam from a three days' tour of the zone. It was a run of more than three hours from our last halt back to Potsdam and one of our hosts, a lieutenant-colonel, insisted on accompanying us the whole way back in his car. Whether this was done out of excessive politeness or in order to make sure that we did not dally by the way was not quite clear, but at any rate it was done as though it was the final act of a perfect host. He drove in front of us in his own car, and his 'adjutant', a very young captain, followed in another car.

When we reached our own mess in Potsdam, we naturally hoped that he would stay and take a meal with us, as it was late in the evening and he had a long drive back. He said that he would like to consult his 'adjutant' before accepting the invitation. He came back rather crestfallen and said that he could not stay.

'What a pity', we remarked. 'However—come in and have a drink at any rate, both you and your adjutant, before you go. We will not delay you more than five minutes.' The poor man evidently thought that this sounded tempting after his drive, but once more he said that he must just 'consult his adjutant'. Back he came, very sheepishly, and told us that the 'adjutant' had reminded him that they had important work to do at headquarters!

Another incident with possibly a grimmer sequel

happened at a big social reception in Moscow, a magnificent party given by the Red Army in honour of their anniversary. Both food and drinks were on a princely scale, and our hosts certainly excelled themselves in hospitality and momentary bonhomie. As a rule the senior official of today is most abstemious, but on this occasion there were some who gave every appearance of having taken full advantage of the sumptuous fare. One of these, a very senior army officer, was particularly effusive in his demonstrations of personal friendship to me, thumping me on the back and 'shooting the usual line' about soldiers being brothers-in-arms, no matter how much the politicians might disagree, and so on. He gave the impression of having had a drink or two 'over the odds', and his conversation was rather loud and indiscreet.

Suddenly he lowered his voice confidentially and said: 'Do you speak German?'

'Hardly at all,' I replied. 'Even worse than Russian, so let us go on as we are doing.' I thought that perhaps he had got the impression that I had been missing some of his pearls of eloquence through imperfect knowledge of the language.

However, ignoring my reply, he switched over to German and began a long story about how he had made contact with both British and Americans during the war, and what fine fellows he thought we both were. Though he began in a stage whisper, the need to make himself audible above the Babel of tongues around us, combined with his slightly alcoholic state, soon overcame his discretion, and he was shouting as loud as before. My own knowledge of

German was inadequate to follow half his ramblings, but I grasped the main theme.

I suddenly noticed a tall, thin officer standing behind my companion, looking away from us with that exaggerated 'far-away' expression common to people who are straining to overhear a conversation without appearing to be listening to it. I tried to cut short my companion's flow of eloquence, but he would not be interrupted. The tall man's interest became more obvious, and I could sense that something was brewing up. There was not long to wait. The tall man tapped my companion on the shoulder and said in an icy tone:

'I do not understand German well. Let us please continue this conversation in Russian.'

The bibulous one gaped open-mouthed and relapsed into a stunned silence. I excused myself with a bow and wandered off to talk to someone else. When I looked about the room a few moments later my German-speaking friend and the tall man had vanished. I did not see them again.

Many of the senior Soviet marshals and generals seemed to be decent, straightforward soldiers of a type with whom, under happier conditions, it might have been possible to form a normal friendship. Some were only uncultured peasants, risen to high positions, but there were one or two who gave the foreign community the impression of having ordinary human ideas on social behaviour. It would not be fair to mention the names of these more 'human' individuals—for their own sakes—but it was pleasant to feel that there were some at least who would like to behave like civilized beings if they dared.

One more episode, though in lighter vein and not connected with the seamy side of M.V.D. activities, is worth recording as an illustration of the tight grip which this organization holds over people in important positions, even in such matters as their 'fun and games' when off duty.

This incident occurred during a huge display of physical culture, given in the Dynamo Stadium on Moscow's 800th anniversary. It was a wonderful performance, some description of which I will give in a later chapter. It was my first experience of one of these big public performances, and I was much intrigued to note how the M.V.D. and ordinary police turned out in immense force to ensure a peaceful afternoon. Each block of spectators in the immense tribune was completely surrounded by a phalanx of blue-and-red caps, who occupied all the gangway seats. I was sitting next to a friendly foreign attaché, and suddenly he tapped me on the knee.

'Do you see that Russian general and his lady, who have just stood up to go?' he said. 'Observe what happens. I think that it will be rather amusing.'

It was nearly the end of the main part of the show, but a rather boring football match was scheduled to wind up the entertainment. In the block of seats immediately to the right of us a Russian general and a lady had just stood up, evidently having decided that they had seen enough for their own enjoyment. They reached the living barrier of

M.V.D. at the end of their row and tried to pass. A very junior M.V.D. officer said something to the general, who seemed to expostulate mildly. Then he and the lady returned to their seats looking guilty and foolish, like a couple of small schoolboys caught slipping away from watching a house-match. It was my first glimpse of 'freedom', as it exists under the M.V.D., and it made me think a little. I tried to imagine what a London coster-monger would say, and do, if a 'bobby' tried to stop him and his girl from leaving Wembley whenever he liked.

Besides the M.V.D. itself there exists the ordinary police or 'militia', but the M.V.D. rules the roost and the ordinary police take their orders implicitly. The same holds good for the huge corps of 'factory guards' and 'watchmen'. Every industrial activity, small or large, has its own special posse of security police. All are armed. All act as a supplement to the M.V.D. The Moscow-Volga Canal, for example, has its own uniformed corps of guards, wearing a semi-naval uniform and armed with rifles.

Thus, quite apart from the ordinary police or 'militia', there can scarcely be an acre of the urban regions which has not got its little posse of armed men, ready to do the work of the M.V.D. As to the ordinary police, one of the first and strongest impressions that the newly arrived foreigner gets is that there is a policeman at every corner of every street. It is almost impossible to lose sight of them. These ordinary police also, both men and women, are armed, and are entirely at the beck and call of the M.V.D.

It can be realized how this sinister body has got the entire country in its grip. It can hush up one incident or fake another with the greatest of ease. Inconvenient witnesses can be suppressed; other 'witnesses' can be produced in unlimited numbers to prove any required story. All public services are entirely under their orders. If the M.V.D. does not wish you to leave Moscow by road, police patrols appear on all the roads to tell you that the roads are 'closed for repairs'. They could just as easily shoot you then and there by the roadside and 'get away with it'. If they wish to prevent you from going to Leningrad (for example) by train, the railway booking-office will tell you, with regret, that no accommodation is available on the train. They will tell you this night after night till you get tired of asking, oblivious of the fact that it is a palpable lie to you and to them.

Such immense power as this, even in the hands of just and honourable men, would be a terrible thing for any country. But when this power is in the hands of some of the lowest and most inhuman types in the nation, the effects upon the whole character of the nation can be appalling. It stands to reason that a service such as the M.V.D. is bound to draw most of its recruits from the sub-human, the sadistic, and the morally warped members of the population. It cannot be a good thing for the soul and character of a great nation that decent self-respecting men and women should have to live in constant dread of these criminal types, or should have to 'kow-tow' to them, knowing themselves to be completely in their power.

There must be something wrong with a system of society which still, after thirty years in power, has to rely upon such a degrading and horrible machine as this to keep its own people in order. Are not the 'blessings' of Communism sufficient to keep the people happy and law-abiding?

CHAPTER VII

LOCAL COLOUR

IN this chapter I intend to select from my diary certain incidents and personal contacts in the hope of giving those who do not know the Russians a first-hand insight into their peculiarities.

It is hard to know where to begin, for although the whole atmosphere behind the Iron Curtain is strange to the westerner, the general effect is one of drab monotony. This applies equally to one's contacts with Soviet officials and to one's travels about the country districts or the suburban slums. When once you have met two or three Soviet officials it is tantamount to having met them all, so little is individuality allowed to show itself.

When you have done half a dozen walks in the country round Moscow, it is unlikely that further walks will show you anything new in the way of scenery or village life. So, although my diary contains accounts of contacts with many officials, no useful purpose would be served by describing more than one or two of them. Though it holds detailed notes of many a country or suburban walk, the individual incidents differentiating one walk from another were often so small as to be of interest only to myself. It was by gradual piecing together of many trivial items rather than by lighting upon any one specially thrilling discovery that I formed a composite picture of social conditions.

Even the 'incidents' of sleuthing and M.V.D. intimidation which frequently enlivened these walks and motor drives themselves ran very closely to type. There were walks on which I managed to free myself of followers. There were others where I noticed them stalking me. Sometimes on these occasions they contented themselves with a childish game of 'hide and seek'. At other times they would engineer some unpleasantness, which might often have the effect of keeping me kicking my heels in some dreary hovel for hours on end.

When the sleuths were on my track I did not, of course, talk to the villagers, because this would only have brought trouble upon innocent peasants. But whenever I felt certain that the sleuths had lost my trail I used to stop at some village *chainaya* (tea-hovel) for a cup of tea, and on all such occasions I met with friendliness and candour.

There was never anything to eat in these hovels (except on one occasion when I was offered a raw carrot!) and the tea was so weak as to be almost colourless hot water. Once or twice I was warned in a friendly way not to stay too long in some particular village because the *Cheka* were very active there. I was always particularly careful not to 'out-stay my welcome' wherever there seemed a risk that my presence might get people into trouble. It always had to be remembered that these people were committing a criminal offence in talking to me at all. Needless to say, I made no attempt to conceal my identity as a foreigner. My accent and general appearance were enough in themselves to advertise this to all concerned, but, to remove all chance of error, I always began by proclaiming my nationality. It was only fair to these poor people.

In the really remote villages far from any motor road and only approachable by a rough un-metalled forest track, the people were far more bold and friendly. Even in these places, however, it was customary for one person to keep watch at the door, evidently to guard against the arrival of someone whom the others did not trust.

I had to be particularly careful to keep the conversation to harmless subjects, against which no reasonable government could have any objection. There was always the possibility of an *agent-provocateur* being planted among these apparently simple peasants with the object of leading the talk into dangerous channels, so as to 'frame' a charge of espionage. Once or twice I encountered people, even in most remote villages, who gave me the feeling that there was danger in talking to them. They usually tended to give themselves away by over-anxiety to bring the talk round to certain subjects.

I was not interested in such subjects. Indeed I was very anxious to avoid them. The more assiduous the sleuthing became, the more anxious I naturally became to do nothing at all which would justify the authorities in their attitude of suspicion and hostility. I was interested merely in the ordinary conditions of life of the villagers and slum-dwellers, and steadfastly resisted all efforts by chance acquaintances to lead on to other less innocent topics. It was sometimes very difficult to maintain this attitude, for the industrial plants of Russia are so widely dispersed over the rural areas that, in the Moscow district at any rate, it is very hard to do a country walk without stumbling upon some factory tucked away in the forest. I used to avoid trying to talk to the people of any village near such a factory, for this of course could have been construed into an attempt to probe its industrial secrets. In any case the real peasants of the unspoiled country districts were far more interesting and pleasant than the industrial proletariat.

Apart from the various M.V.D. 'incidents' that were aimed at me personally, there were only three occasions during my walks when I witnessed trouble between police and the ordinary people.

The most important of these was quite exciting, though I did not think it wise to hang about in idle curiosity for too long. I had taken the electric train to Balaschicka, a small town ten miles or so east of Moscow, and was walking back into the suburbs. As I reached the outer industrial slums I noticed something going on round a block of tenements a couple of hundred yards off my road. There was a big crowd standing about, and I could see over the heads of the crowd the red and blue caps of the M.V.D. A group of working-class women were coming away from the crowd, weeping and wailing.

I joined the crowd and craned my neck to see what was going on. There was a cordon of M.V.D. completely surrounding the block of buildings. They had brought some lorries with them, and in one of these a few dejected civilian men were sitting with more M.V.D. guarding them. There were ordinary police there too, but they were mainly occupied in trying to move the crowd of spectators on. Every time that the police officer shouted at one

115

section of the crowd, that part of the crowd began to slink off hurriedly, but all the time new-comers from other directions kept swelling the numbers on the other side of the square.

I did not dare to ask what was happening, for it might have been something that a foreigner was not supposed to see. From scraps of talk among those near me, I gathered that a search was going on, and that the demeanour of the spectators was sullenly hostile but very frightened. After I had watched proceedings for a few minutes the ordinary police began pushing their way into the crowd, belabouring spectators with their truncheons. The crowd dispersed hurriedly. I followed their example.

The next incident, though trivial, was interesting as an illustration of the fact that the police do not always get the better of things, even in police-infested Moscow. I was in the big square in front of the Kurski railway station when I saw a policeman (militia, not M.V.D.) questioning an old peasant woman. She was evidently on her way to catch a train, and was carrying a few old bits of cloth rolled into a ragged bundle.

The policeman had compelled her to unroll the bundle and spread it out for his inspection. There seemed to be something wrong, for when I first saw the couple the policeman had got hold of the old woman by the arm and was trying to drag her away, having taken charge of the bundle and tucked it under his other arm. The old woman started shrieking, and tried to throw herself on the ground to resist removal.

A crowd quickly gathered, for the Kurski station

116

approach is usually swarming with country people. It was
obvious that the sympathy of the crowd was with the old
woman. Encouraged by this moral support, she redoubled
her lamentations, pouring out a stream of abuse against the
policeman. A colleague joined him, but the two of them
were soon surrounded by a large and muttering crowd.
For once in a way no further reinforcements of police
were within immediate call. Both police blew their
whistles loudly and long, but the crowd was making too
much din and the rumble of traffic helped to drown the
sound of whistling.

The police were both young men and perhaps inexperi-
enced. They tried to force their way through the crowd,
dragging their prisoner, but the people, without actually
barring the way, still contrived to make progress very
difficult. Meanwhile the old lady screamed abuse and made
herself as heavy and awkward a burden as possible. One
policeman drew his revolver, but lacked the courage to do
more than wave it vaguely at the crowd. There was nobody
who seemed to be a leader. There was no overt opposition
at all on the part of the crowd. There was simply a passive
hostility, masquerading perhaps as peasant stupidity, but
none the less strong enough to make itself felt. In the end
the policemen, after whispering anxiously together,
released their hold on the old woman and shambled off
sheepishly through the crowd, who now parted readily to
let them go through and grinned exultantly behind their
backs. The old woman, at first scarcely able to believe her
escape, hastily rolled up her bundle of rags, which the
policeman had dropped in the scuffle, and made off in

another direction, muttering savagely. The crowd itself lost no time in dispersing, evidently afraid that the police might soon return in greater strength. This was by no means the only occasion when I saw signs of latent hostility toward the police, though as a rule it never got further than black looks and grumbles.

The third case happened in the untidy slum which lies round the great Saratov gas works toward the Ryazan road. It was during the height of the bread shortage, just before the dismissal of Liubimov. The bread queues had been growing longer every day, and on this particular occasion one of these queues was evidently the origin of the trouble. I was in a tram when I first noticed something peculiar. Several lorry loads of police passed us, and a car load of M.V.D. officers. Presently we passed a side street which was crammed with a huge crowd of very poor people, mostly women. The place was alive with police also. Two or three lorries had stopped and were disembarking new police reinforcements. I alighted and strolled along the side street to see what was happening.

The centre of excitement was a baker's shop, outside which stood the longest queue that I had so far seen. It was clear that the disturbance, whatever it may have been, which had necessitated this considerable show of police force was now over. A cold rain was falling and the crowd looked dejected and miserable, but quite subdued and orderly. I was so intrigued to know what it was all about that I broke my usual rule of discretion and asked one of the bystanders.

"No bread," she muttered in disgust. Then, noting the

obvious fact that I was a foreigner, she continued more cautiously: 'Nichevo. There was a little difficulty, but it will be all right now, I think."

'How long have you been waiting here?' I asked.

'Myself only since this morning. But those—' pointing toward the head of the queue, 'many are here since last night.' It was then mid-afternoon.

It must not be supposed that such excitements were to be found every day. Many a walk and many a motor drive I did with nothing to break the monotony of the rather dreary countryside except the childish antics and man-œuvres of my sleuths. Whether on foot, when I did a walk, or in a car, when I drove out in my own, their technique was always the same—the same elaborate but unsuccessful efforts to conceal their presence, which efforts still per-sisted even when I had shown them clearly that I knew that they were there. The most ridiculous case of all happened in April, when the snow, though still deep, was beginning to melt off the roads. We set out along a main road running north-east from Moscow, intending to do a round by the town of Krasnoarmeisk and back by the Zagorsk road. In actual fact the paucity of roads fit for cars is such that it is practically impossible, within a single day's motor drive, to go out by one road and come back by another.

On this particular occasion it was the snow that turned us back. Lorry traffic had worn two deep ruts along the road, but the clearance of my car was inadequate to ride over the central ridge of hard snow. Our sleuths were evidently in a similar plight, though they enjoyed the slight advantage of following in our path.

Just round a bend in the road we ran into a deep drift and there we stuck. The sleuths had been hanging back in their usual manner, fondly imagining no doubt that they had not been seen. A moment after we had become stuck in the snow they also rounded the bend, only with difficulty pulling up just behind us. The driver lost his head and tried to back their car hurriedly out of sight again round the corner. He was much too hasty. One of his back wheels left the hard road and slipped into a deep ditch. There they remained, even more firmly bogged than our own car, and only a few yards from us.

Each party struggled for a while to free its own car, each feigning to ignore the presence of any other car on the road. An ever-growing queue of lorries began to form on each side of the double obstruction.

United effort being obviously the right answer to our common misfortune, we finally suggested to the sleuths that we should pool our man-power and concentrate upon each car in turn. We further suggested that they should use their M.V.D. authority to co-opt the help of the waiting lorry drivers, since these showed no inclination to lift a finger voluntarily to help to clear the road for themselves.

The sleuths seemed slightly confused at being engaged in friendly conversation by the people who were being stalked, but after a short hesitation they fell in with our suggestion. In a very short time both cars were mobile again, and in due course, after some traffic control by the

British element, the two columns of traffic managed to squeeze past one another on the narrow road.

During the process of un-ditching the cars I talked quite amicably with the principal sleuth, and asked his advice as to whether we could get round to the Zagorsk road. We made it clear to him that we would be only too pleased in future to keep him informed of our intended journeys, if only he would openly make contact with us at the beginning of each day's run. He agreed that this would simplify his work quite a lot and would be more satisfactory and dignified for all concerned. However, in spite of this 'breaking of the ice' between us, matters went on in just the same childish manner as before.

It was often hard to imagine what the authorities hoped to gain by these tactics. On another occasion, after this affair on the snow-bound road, a party of us set off by car one day to picnic by the River Volga near the town of Ivanovo, where the Moscow-Volga Canal has its northern terminus. The road to Ivanovo passes through another small town, Dmitrov, roughly half-way, and for the last twenty or thirty miles to Ivanovo there is no other turning off the road.

It must, therefore, have been quite obvious to our sleuths, when once we had passed through Dmitrov, that we were heading for Ivanovo and the Volga. It would have been a simple matter for them to have overtaken us and warned us that this particular road was closed ahead of us. They did nothing of the kind. It was not till we got within a mile or so of the Volga that our road was barred by an

121

armed sentry in the uniform of the special canal police. Considerable time and petrol could have been saved, both for our sleuths and ourselves, if they had warned us twenty miles or so earlier. Was it just stupidity, or deliberate malice, or a strange lack of liaison between the canal police and the M.V.D. which prevented them from taking this common-sense action? The ways of the M.V.D. sleuths were often beyond comprehension.

I have mentioned the lack of initiative of the lorry drivers, who seemed content to sit indefinitely in their lorries waiting for others to open a road for them. This lack of initiative was once exhibited in an even more startling form when I was motoring in the Soviet Zone of Germany.

We had set out very early one morning to do a long day's run, and it was still dark as we drove down the Leipzig *Autobahn*. We saw someone waving a lantern ahead and pulled up. There was a Russian military convoy of about twenty lorries, halted without lights. An officer asked if we could help him. They had all run out of petrol!

We explained that we had not enough spare petrol to make much difference to so many vehicles, but offered to give the officer, or anyone that he cared to send with us, a lift as far as the next Soviet 'Kommandatura', where, no doubt, he would be able to arrange a fresh supply for the whole convoy. The officer hesitated, then declined our offer with thanks. He had perhaps expected to stop a Russian car, and was rather taken aback at finding himself dealing with foreigners.

'Could we take any message on for him?' we asked. No. He thought that perhaps the best thing for him to do would be to wait for orders. So we drove on.

The following night at about ten o'clock or later (i.e., more than sixteen hours after the morning's incident) we passed that way again on our way home. The convoy was still there. The officer was still standing in the road, waiting for orders.

It is hard to reconcile military methods of that kind with the undoubted fact that Soviet staff work, on what our own army calls 'the Q side', must have worked with considerable efficiency during the recent war. The answer probably lies in the fact that the Soviet soldier is an oriental, who can get along after a fashion and fight well with a lack of administrative amenities which would be bad for the efficiency of more civilized men. I do not know what was in those lorries on the Leipzig *Autobahn*. Let us suppose that it may have been rations for some unit. The unit may have had to go hungry for another twenty hours. What matter?

This callousness toward the individual soldier and the toughness of that same soldier were demonstrated by another incident in the Soviet Zone. On one of our tours through the Zone, a British car was involved in an accident and badly damaged. I went to the 'Kommand-atura' at Stendal, the nearest town, to ask for a Soviet guard to be posted on the vehicle till we could collect it next morning. After some delay, quite long enough to have turned out a properly equipped guard, two young

123

private soldiers were produced, each with a rifle and nothing else—no greatcoat, no blanket, no rations. It was late in November and bitterly cold at night.

An officer came along with us to the wrecked vehicle to give the sentries their orders. On the way I asked him whether the soldiers had had a meal before starting.

'I have no idea,' he replied. 'Why?'

In reply to further questions he explained to me that it would be the duty of both these sentries to remain awake all night. They would remain on duty till some unspecified hour next day, whenever the British should see fit to retrieve the wrecked car. They were then to march back to Stendal, a matter of about ten miles, and rejoin their unit.

This callousness about minor comforts for individuals is reflected in a corresponding light-heartedness about human life. I was walking one day in the wooded and lakeland country round Werder when suddenly there was a crackle of machine-gun fire, and chips began to fly from the trees round about me. I took cover behind the thickest trunk nearby, very puzzled and rather alarmed.

There were villages dotted about those woods and quite a large number of Germans, men and women, working in the fields and forest close about me.

Fortunately the fusillade soon ceased, so I walked on with the intention of getting clear of the place as soon as I could. I had not gone far before the countryside was sprayed again. This happened two or three times before I got into the open and was able to see what was happening.

Three little light aeroplanes of very slow flight were manœuvring overhead, only a couple of hundred feet or so above the trees. One was towing a target and the other two were shooting at it. It did not seem to matter to anybody that between them they were spraying several square miles of inhabited territory, containing not only German villages, but many Russian soldiers also, and at least two motor roads.

The Soviet soldier himself, in spite of this apparent lack of regard for his welfare, is on the whole a cheerful and likeable individual—considerably more likeable, in fact, than many of his seniors. They frequently used to stop us to ask for lifts on the roads of Germany, and displayed no hostility, suspicion, or fear of friendly conversation, when they discovered that they had got into a British car. Taking my combined experiences in Germany and Russia together I can say as a general rule that the more lowly the individual, and the further he is from Moscow or Potsdam, the more human and pleasant the Soviet citizen becomes.

Even in Potsdam there was a degree of friendly contact with certain Soviet officers which in retrospect seemed almost cordial to me when compared to the leprous isolation of Moscow. It would not be fair to mention names, but several more junior officers of the Potsdam garrison showed that they at any rate wished to be friendly, no matter how their superior officers at headquarters might behave. We never quite knew who might 'blow in'

125

to our mess near Sans Souci. We never quite knew if these chance callers were all that they represented themselves to be, or whether there was anything behind their seemingly careless bonhomie. One instance out of many will suffice.

We were just going to bed one evening when a clatter of hooves was heard outside the mess. Next moment in came a young Russian officer, a cavalryman. He was 'roaring drunk', or at any rate acted as though he were. One can never be quite sure.

We welcomed him, of course, and offered him a chair and a smoke. It seemed like 'carrying coals to Newcastle' to offer him a drink, but it would have been churlish and insulting not to, so we offered him that too. He accepted everything with alacrity, and settled down in one of our good armchairs, apparently bent upon making a night of it.

After he had polished off several drinks and had sung a few Russian songs, he started to get maudlin and careless in his talk. We glanced at one another with the same thought in our minds—'Was it a trick?'

Lest we should seem to have been uncharitably suspicious in this matter it should be remembered that next door to our mess was the local headquarters of the green-capped frontier guards, who performed the same functions in Germany that their colleagues, the M.V.D., perform on Soviet territory proper. It was extremely unlikely that anyone ever visited our mess without the knowledge, if not the connivance, of our neighbours.

The night wore on and our guest began to get drowsy. So did we! We dropped one or two broad hints, suggesting that his horse might be getting cold waiting outside. He scorned this idea, boasting that Russian horses were tough and did not have to be molly-coddled. We asked him whether he lived far from our mess, and was he sure that he knew the way home? He replied that he himself neither knew it or cared. His horse knew the way home! What else was a horse for?

At last someone had a brain-wave and began to praise the world-famous horsemanship of the Russian cavalry. We had never had a chance of seeing the real thing. Would he very kindly show us a thing or two? He swallowed the bait at once and we all went outside, where a shaggy little brown cob was standing patiently awaiting his master. We felt no qualms in letting this drunken man mount, because it was obvious that he was a born horseman and could come to no harm in the saddle, drunk or sober. We were trusting to the homing instincts of his charger to get him to his own barracks safely. We rather imagined that, once in the saddle, he would let the cob take charge and we would be rid of him.

Not a bit of it! He remembered well enough what we had come out to see—a 'rodeo'. Very well then, a 'rodeo' we should see. Our courtyard was paved with smooth slippery slabs, not at all a suitable manège for tricks of equitation even in daylight, much less at night. But this did not worry the Russian. He stood the cob on his hind legs, then spun him round two or three times with his hooves striking sparks from the paving stones. Then he was off in a mad gallop round our small and slippery courtyard. At every corner we expected horse and rider to

127

come down, but all was well. As he passed in front of the mess he vaulted in and out of the saddle two or three times from both sides of the horse. It was too dark to see what happened at the far end of the yard, but suddenly we heard a fresh sound. They had jumped the small gate at the far end and were cantering away down the hard high road. Mr Jorrocks would have been horrified, but to us the sound of his clattering hooves receding into the distance was a sheer joy. We were rid of him at last!

Quickly we shut up the mess and dispersed to bed, fearing that he might change his mind and come back. I had hardly put my head on the pillow when I heard a familiar sound again—the clatter of hooves outside the mess. Then came a deafening rattle on the front door and a voice began singing 'Stenka Razin' sadly out of tune. I lay still. The lights of the mess were all out. I hoped that nobody would be foolish enough to succumb to over-punctilious hospitality. All was well. Nobody was foolish.

Next morning, apart from the usual traces of a horse, there was nothing to show that our visitor had been more than a dream. We never saw or heard of him again.

With the more senior officers at Marshal Sokolovsky's headquarters we never quite knew how we stood. If they promised anything at all, which was rare, they often recanted afterwards, or perhaps someone still higher reversed the decision. There was, for example, the curious affair of the Potsdam Officers' Club. A certain Colonel Zorrin (there can be no harm in mentioning his name for the poor man has no doubt already suffered for his kind act) was at first our liaison officer. He told us that there would be no objection at all to our making use of the officers' club, and the other amenities in the 'Park of Culture and Rest' wherein the club was situated. Several of us went there without meeting with any unpleasantness, and enjoyed the cinema shows and other entertainments. Suddenly one evening there was an 'incident'.

I was not present myself on this occasion. Apparently a general, not normally stationed at headquarters, took a strong objection to the presence of British officers. He became most offensive and insisted upon their immediate departure, sending a junior officer to see them off the premises. Naturally we never went there again. Colonel Zorrin was shortly afterwards recalled to Moscow. We never met him again.

Most of our dealings thereafter were with a Major-General Lavrentiev, who certainly did not err on the side of excessive co-operation. He was a typical 'poker-face'. He wore a perpetual smile, which disclosed a mouthful of gold teeth. He was never rude. On the other hand we very soon got to know that his benign smile meant precisely nothing at all. He belonged to a special class of Soviet officer, whose speciality is dealing with foreign officers. When you have met one you have met them all.

Major-General Seraev, my only link with officialdom in Moscow, was another of the same type. A short, round, little man with a clean-shaven face that at first seemed genial and kindly, his speciality was skill in avoiding the giving of a straight answer. I wrote five letters to him during my year in Moscow, to which I never received any answer whatsoever. The first of these was written within a week of my arrival. As his office was five minutes' walk from mine, one can hardly call this cordial liaison as practised by civilized nations. When, toward the end of my stay in Moscow, I remonstrated with him about these five unanswered letters, he wrote me a most offensive letter of abuse. Yet, when I met him at cocktail parties or other similar occasions, he was as cordial as a senior Russian dares to be. I always felt that he was playing a part, and would like to have been less unpleasant than he was forced officially to be. In this I may perhaps have misjudged him.

A far less pleasant individual was Captain Pasko, a naval officer on General Seraev's staff. He was the officer concerned in the 'affair of the sheepskin coat'. Though it lay within his power to have settled the whole matter merely by mentioning the fact that I had asked him to search me, he persisted in remaining silent. He deliberately lied to me in pretending that we were to see General Seraev that night, on leaving the factory. It should be remembered that, till then, I had regarded him as a decent and honourable man, almost as a personal friend. He had enough sense of shame to avoid me thereafter on cocktail party occasions. It was amusing in a contemptuous way to watch him oiling out of sight among the crowd. In appearance he was rather insignificant with a face of most extraordinary pallor, almost dead white. I dare say that even he could not help his treacherous behaviour, but it went rather against the grain to see a sailor mixed up in such dirty work.

Fortunately they were not all as bad as that. In the Soviet Zone of Germany, particularly at a distance from Potsdam, we frequently met senior officers who did their best to behave as ordinary civilized human beings. In all cases these were 'genuine' soldiers, not 'political officers'. There was usually one of the latter type attached to each staff, and relations never succeeded in becoming entirely nformal or friendly while this individual was about. These 'political officers' run very much to type. After a little practice it is easy to distinguish them, almost at a glance, from the 'genuine' soldiers, even though they no longer carry any special designation nor do they wear any distinctive uniform.

Russian hospitality has often been described by others. In our tours of the Soviet Zone we experienced official hospitality in lavish form. Provincial governors and commandants of the big towns as a rule left nothing undone to entertain us. Many of these officers showed that they understood the true art of being a good host, and realized that there was something more in it than the mere quantity of food and drink provided. It would not be fair to these more courteous officers to single out particular names as examples of friendly behaviour. A short account of a typical night's halt, as guests of a local governor, may perhaps be of interest.

Hospitality always began with an enormous banquet, which started as soon as possible after our arrival. We were ushered into a large room, in which was a long table, loaded to capacity with cold viands of many varieties and bottles of vodka or cognac (or both) in serried ranks

131

down the table. Immediately we were seated, the ritual of toast-drinking began. It is a formidable business, calling for tactful but absolutely firm refusal on the part of the foreign guest at a certain stage in the string of toasts. A lot of nonsense has been uttered about the alleged necessity of drinking 'level' with one's Russian hosts for fear of giving offence. Certainly many an host, particularly one of the less pleasant 'political' type, will make a great show of feigning umbrage if his guest refuses to drink beyond a certain point. Beware of any host who takes this line, for it is part of a regular technique for getting foreigners off their guard. One can be safe in assuming that any host who takes that line and insists upon it is playing a dirty game and abusing the true spirit of hospitality. If you watch such an host carefully, it will frequently be observed that his vodka is poured out of a different bottle to that of his guests. Vodka and water are very similar in outward appearance!

The more honest and genuine type of host rarely evinces surprise or umbrage when his guest indicates firmly that he has reached his limit of toast-drinking. It is, in fact, almost a sure criterion whereby the true host can be distinguished from the false. Russians know better than anybody that it is only an exceptional foreigner who can drink vodka 'level' with those who have been brought up to it from the cradle. They merely regard anyone who tries to do so as a fool who has not the moral courage to acknowledge this.

But real firmness will be required before the constant replenishment of glasses is definitely brought to an end. It is an essential formality of Russian toast-drinking that there must be 'no heel-taps', and it is as well to conform to this punctilio.

As soon as the empty glass is set down, an orderly will silently appear behind your shoulder and endeavour to fill it up again. It is at that point that the polite but firm line must be taken, and maintained, no matter how insulted one's host pretends to be.

Another useful tip in the technique of drinking vodka without ill effect is to eat something *immediately* after the glass of vodka has gone down. It will be noted that one's host and his staff always do this. I have included this brief essay on the art of Russian toast-drinking because one day perhaps the Iron Curtain may be drawn aside sufficiently for business men, and others from the West, to make contacts with their Soviet counterparts. Adherence to these simple rules may save many a beginner, not only from a sore head, but from getting the worst of a bargain or perhaps letting his tongue run away with him.

To return to the banquet. It is advisable not to let one's appetite go too freely upon the wealth of cold viands waiting on the table to be eaten. On our first experience of this kind in Germany we were badly caught. We had arrived rather later than intended owing to trouble on the road, and we jumped to the conclusion that our hosts, in view of this delay, had provided a lavish cold buffet instead of a hot meal. We had good cause to think so, because, among other delicacies such as caviare, smoked salmon, and sausages, three roasted sucking-pigs adorned the table, served complete, heads and all. So we fell to and

133

made a hearty meal of these substantial dishes. To our horror, just as we began to think that it was nearly time to leave the table, a file of orderlies marched in with steaming plates of soup, the fore-runners of a five-course dinner!

The reader may have difficulty in reconciling this tale of gargantuan repasts with the grim picture of want among the poor non-official people of Russia. The explanation is that food is a weapon of Soviet propaganda, to be lavished or refused just as it happens to suit the totalitarian plan.

When at last dinner was over, arrangements were made to keep us amused till it was time to go to bed. Here again could be found a difference between hosts who were genuine and those who were playing a deeper game. The former used to entertain us as intelligently as local resources allowed—seats at the opera in some of the larger German towns, or, failing that, a display of Russian dances by their own people. The more sinister type of host often tried to provide female company for the younger and more susceptible members of our party and still more drink for the crusty old veterans.

Breakfast was usually rather an ordeal, for it was often an exact replica of the previous night's banquet. It was rather a shock, even for the hardest-headed among us, on entering the dining-room before an early start on our journey, to find the table once more garnished with bottles of vodka and cognac and laden with what remained of last night's cold viands.

This description of Soviet hospitality in their zone of Germany may clash strangely with what I have written elsewhere about the social ostracism meted out to the diplomatic community in Moscow. I have included it for that very purpose. Certainly it does seem incongruous, contradictory, and illogical. I felt this very strongly myself the following year, when I got to Moscow and found how we were all treated as unapproachable lepers. It seemed scarcely credible that Soviet officialdom could behave in two such entirely different ways. But the important point is that they do. It is a point that ought to be more clearly appreciated by distinguished individuals of our own or other nations who meet with official Soviet hospitality for the first time. Far too many such people have come away from such brief encounters, complacently convinced that the Russians are 'not such bad fellows after all' and that 'they only need a bit of understanding' or 'talking to as man to man'. A little knowledge is a dangerous thing. It is quite true that the ordinary *non-official* Russian is at heart 'not such a bad fellow'. He is, in fact, a very likeable character. The trouble is that he is so rarely allowed to give rein to his better nature.

Cynical and ungrateful as it may sound to say so, it is unfortunately a fact that *official* Soviet hospitality must, under present circumstances, be taken with a big pinch of salt as a part of the game of politics and propaganda. It used to provide us with a salutary corrective, after an evening such as I have described, to drive next day through the German countryside. It was not that we often came upon anything sensational in the way of horrors any more than I did a year later on many of my walks round

135

Moscow. In both cases there was a similar air of dreary hopelessness mingled with constant fear. You might travel many miles in both lands without happening upon any tangible reason for this fear. It was only once, I am thankful to say, that I came upon a slave camp in nearly a year of wandering about the backwoods of the Moscow province. It was only once during a year of touring through the Soviet Zone of Germany that I personally saw something similar there.

We were motoring near Dessau at the time. The nearest village, Apollendorf, was some distance away. We came upon a barbed-wire camp of orthodox type—double apron fence, watch-towers, and lights all complete. It was empty, but, as we approached it, a passenger train came from the other direction and halted near the camp. There was no station there nor even a platform—just a single line running through the forest. Several hundred male German civilians alighted, and with them were armed German police. Each civilian carried a small roll of personal clothing. They were marshalled by the police and started walking over toward the enclosed camp.

I do not know who or what they were. It was not our business to enquire. They may all have been convicted Nazis for all we knew. But they certainly could not have been very prominent Nazis. They were obviously very ordinary working men; not by any stretch of imagination were they leaders. The train was heading east. Whatever the explanation may be, it is a fact, for which I can vouch by personal observation, that behind the Iron Curtain, both on Soviet territory and off it, people were still being rounded up by the hundred, two and three years after the war, and were being herded wholesale like cattle into pens.

Mention of my visits to village *chainayas* earlier in this chapter may perhaps have given some readers the impression that the rural population has plenty of leisure to enjoy rest, pleasant talk, and a cup of tea in some sort of an equivalent to the village inn of England. Such an impression would be wrong.

These places are dirty hovels of no comfort whatsoever. Because they happen to be situated near the centre of a village, and because most villages boast no other kind of a meeting place at all, it often happens that these hovels provide a rendezvous where two men may meet for a brief talk while they pass through the village on their various jobs. Nobody has leisure to stay there very long, except of course in the winter, when the snow is on the ground and there is not so much to do in the fields and forests.

In that respect at least the rural peasantry are better off than the industrial proletariat of Russia. Agriculture, being dependent upon the seasons, is not so susceptible to the disguised slave-driving methods of 'stakhanovism' and 'norms' as is the work of town-dwellers. This does not, however, deter the Soviet authorities from trying to exploit such methods in agriculture.

It is quite common to find a notice-board outside the village *chainaya* whereon are posted notices belauding some *kolhoz* or other for having exceeded its 'norm' during the past season by some phenomenal percentage. Most villages of any size have their 'shock brigadiers', whose job it is to bully or encourage the peasants to produce ever more and more work out of every twenty-four hours. Besides this, in the country districts nearer to Moscow itself, agriculture and industry are so closely interwoven that many villages support both a factory and a *kolhoz* (collective farm).

The principle of 'stakhanovism' has been fully described in other books on Russia. All that I can add from personal observation is that it is undoubtedly extremely unpopular among the workers, no matter what its value may be in increasing the national output. This is only natural. It is one thing for some young athlete, rewarded for his prowess with extra rations, to go about the country demonstrating how to cut (say) double the normal quota of coal in a given time. He only keeps this rate up for a short spurt, then away he goes to be lauded and fêted somewhere else. But the inevitable result of his exploits will be that the 'norm' fixed for ordinary under-nourished workers keeps on being set ever higher and higher. It is not surprising that these national heroes of industry are not really as popular among the rank-and-file of their fellow workers as they are made out to be in the columns of the Soviet press.

The nearest urban equivalent to the village *chainaya* is the pavement booth for the sale of beer, minerals and vodka. At these uninviting state-owned 'pubs' the complete absence of any comfort whatsoever is enough to discourage even that short dalliance over a drink which is sometimes indulged in the village hovel. Customers just queue up for their glass and gulp it down hastily on the pavement in the snow or rain, then move on without talking to their fellows. Not only would it be uncomfortable but it is also dangerous to air one's views to strangers in the town. So it comes about that it was rare indeed to hear candid views on 'stakhanovism' from an urban industrial worker. This reticence, however, was more than made up by the outspoken opinions expressed in the smaller country towns and in the villages.

This chapter will have achieved its object if it gives the reader a glimpse of 'local colour' behind the Iron Curtain. The superficial and often false bonhomie of Soviet officials on first acquaintance—that is an experience that many must have had, though many do not probe deep enough to discover how little of real value lies behind it. The impression of drab monotony—that also anyone can obtain who takes the trouble to go about with his eyes open in Communist-ruled lands. The sense of fear is equally easy to observe, though one may travel many an uneventful day's journey without happening upon any tangible cause for fear. But, in order to see the truth, *unaccompanied* travel is necessary. Those who put themselves into the kind hands of official hosts and guides are not likely to get beyond the first stage—the wonderfully lavish hospitality of Soviet officialdom.

CHAPTER VIII

THE LIGHTER SIDE OF SOVIET LIFE

AS the ship left Helsinki on my way to Russia, there was a yacht race in progress just outside the harbour, and we had to give way to allow twenty or thirty 'Dragons' to cross our bow, close-hauled to a fresh easterly breeze and keeping very well together. It was a beautiful sight. As we watched them pass, one of my fellow-travellers, a foreign diplomat returning to Moscow after his leave, remarked:

'Take a good look at them. It is about the last time that you will see grown-up people enjoying any spontaneous fun for many a long day.' The word 'spontaneous' made his criticism of Russia quite a fair one.

There is plenty of fun of a sort in the Soviet Union, but it is all highly organized. For those who like to take their recreation in tabloid form this may be satisfactory, but there is no scope for individual taste or personal initiative. It is not possible, for example, to plan one's own holiday or the family holiday as normal people would do in England. One cannot just go off to the seaside or to the mountains, or even to friends in the country, without formality or fuss. It is necessary to get the whole thing organized through one's place of work—the factory, or the *kolhoz*, or, if you are an official of any kind, through the appropriate ministry. It is necessary to submit your application well in advance, and in due course you may be allotted a vacancy in one of the so-called 'sanatoria', which are a feature of this state-run annual holiday scheme.

These 'sanatoria' are a cross between a holiday camp and a convalescent home. In spite of the name it is not necessary to be ill to be admitted to a sanatorium. A certificate is probably required from the factory doctor to state that you are in need of a rest, but of that I am not sure. There are sanatoria in the Caucasus Mountains and in the pleasant seaside resorts of the Crimea, but these are reserved exclusively for important government officials and their families. There are other sanatoria in the woods round Moscow, particularly in the pleasant lake district about thirty miles north of the capital. There are others on the very edge of Moscow. One's social status in the governmental hierarchy decides the standard of sanatorium to which one is entitled to go.

I managed to visit two of these places during my stay in Moscow, not as an inmate but just for a quick glance round. One was for generals and their wives; the other was for technicians of factories of fairly superior grades. They were quite comfortable after a fashion, but not quite my own idea for a holiday. Personally, I would rather spend my holiday on a walking tour through the forests or a canoe trip down the Volga, but I do not believe that either of these would be approved by the authorities.

Some sanatoria are for men only, others (presumably) for women only, while the higher-grade ones cater for the more exalted officials and their wives in one sanatorium. In the two that I visited there did not appear to be very much to do, except to sit about and eat and drink and play cards, or listen to the wireless, but perhaps things are better in the Crimea and the Caucasus.

Apart from the annual holiday the state sees to it that a certain amount of organized fun is available on state holidays. An invariable feature of such occasions is the display of fireworks and searchlights and the firing of artillery salutes after dark. All this is extremely well organized. There is undoubtedly something in the Russian temperament which lends itself to the stage-management of big public displays. In all these big shows one can see the artistic colour sense of the Slavs at its best, whether it be a massed display of physical culture by daylight or illumination of the city by night.

The celebrations for Moscow's 800th anniversary were, as I mentioned earlier, my first opportunity of seeing one of these state pageants, and it certainly was most impressive. In the Dynamo Stadium during the afternoon, athletic clubs from all over Russia provided teams, totalling many hundreds of young men and women. Their colouring was so chosen that when they posed *en masse* for various set-piece displays, the effect of all the blended colours was really fine. A similar triumph of colour scheme was to be seen that night, when the Red Square was illuminated and the pyrotechnics began. The walls of the Kremlin were picked out in myriads of little lights, which delineated the ancient towers and battlements like the scenery in some beautiful fairy play. Lenin's sombre mausoleum was flood-lit in an eerie mauve light, and beyond it the beautiful church of St Basil, one of the finest buildings in Moscow, looked mysterious in a pale green and yellow glow.

This same flair for artistic colour schemes, which the authorities certainly know how to exploit to the best advantage, is to be seen also in Russian theatrical decors, above all in the ballet.

The ballet is the one thing in Russia today for which there can be nothing but unstinted praise. Like, I suppose, most Englishmen, I neither knew nor cared very much about ballet before going to Moscow. It was an education to me. I had no idea that so much expression could be drawn from the mere actions of moving about the stage without need for a spoken word to tell the story. After seeing Ulanova dancing in *Giselle* at the Bolshoi Theatre it seemed to me that anything else that Russia had to show me must inevitably be an anti-climax. It was time for me to go. It was an experience that I hope I shall never forget.

The 'Devil scene' in *Swan Lake* was another memorable experience, perhaps the scene which illustrates most strongly the Slavonic gift for colour. The eclipse scene in the opera *Prince Igor* also, I think, shows this scenic art to perfection.

Another theatrical entertainment, peculiar to Moscow, was the Puppet Theatre, where the whole play is performed by dolls manipulated by the hands of hidden artists, after the style of a Punch and Judy Show.

There is a great variety of first-class theatrical entertainment to be enjoyed in Moscow. After the infuriating frustrations of trying to make sense of Soviet officialdom during our working hours it was a welcome relief in the

143

evening to be able to feel that at least there were some aspects of Russian life that were still sane and natural and 'human'.

But even in one's moments of relaxation at the theatre the Soviet citizen is not entirely free from the grand-motherly supervision of the state. One evening we went to a performance of folk-dances and similar national entertainment at the Tchaikowsky Hall. As a rule this sort of entertainment was excellent, but on this occasion it seemed to be falling rather flat. Up to the interval the show was definitely a 'flop'. There was a man who kept giving solo performances, and returning at once to give an *encore* on the slightest provocation, even though the applause had definitely been lukewarm. On the other hand there was another turn, some young dancers, who 'brought the house down', yet they were hustled off the stage without a chance of taking an *encore*, though the crowd obviously wanted them back. By the interval it was clear that we were all bored and ready to go home. Just as we were making up our minds, while strolling round we happened to meet a Russian lady of our acquaint-ance and told her candidly what we thought of the show. She did her best to explain that it would improve out of all recognition after the interval.

'You see,' she explained, 'in the first half the manage-ment puts on what the state feels that the people *ought* to enjoy. The idea is to educate the taste of the people. Next time we shall see what the management knows that the people do like.'

She further explained that the gentleman of the frequent

encores, whose performance apparently had been high above the heads of his unregenerate audience, was the winner of a Stalin Prize for music. It would have been most unseemly if the audience had been allowed to show that they really preferred the performance of the troop of young dancers. So, even in their few moments of relaxation, the people of the Soviet Union are guided and shepherded by the state.

Even the allotment of theatre tickets is subject to a great deal of state control. During the first part of my stay in Moscow large blocks of theatre tickets were farmed out to various factories and similar institutions. These institutions used to redistribute them to their workers as rewards for zeal and energy in the performance of their duties. In those days the theatres were always packed. Only a comparatively few seats were set aside for individual sale to members of the foreign diplomatic community or other unprivileged 'lepers'.

This system was abolished and purchase of seats became nominally free for all. The immediate result of this was that for some time theatres played to almost empty houses. The vast audiences who had flocked to them when seats had been given away by factory committees (and paid for by the state) thought twice about going when they had to pay out of their own pockets. It was an interesting demonstration of the limitations of state interference as a means of ramming 'culture' down people's throats.

But even after the abolition of this state dole of seats

the purchase of one's evening entertainment was still not quite free from governmental interference. It was not possible to find out till within a few hours of any given performance whether or no any seats were available. The reason for this irritating arrangement was that at the last moment some member of the Polit-Buro or some other mighty government official might take it into his head to go to the theatre and take a few friends with him. If so the requisite number of private purchasers would have to be disappointed.

If a young Soviet citizen, male or female, shows promise of being a 'star turn' at any particular branch of athletics, he or she will be given opportunities for taking part in that form of athletics. But not otherwise. Everything is organized through the factory club or other suitable club. There is little or no chance of indulging in any game just for the fun of it, unless the authorities consider that you are good enough at it to be a credit to the factory or other community. The idea of a few enthusiasts getting together on their own initiative and starting a village club, even for the simplest games, would be out of the question.

In most other countries, no matter how poor, the village lads usually get together and rig up some sort of facilities for simple local games—e.g. the *hai-alai frontons* (*pelota*) and *bolas* pitches of Northern Spain. It is not a question of poverty or wealth—merely of individual liberty. In the Soviet Union even the individual's spare time is not sufficiently his own for him and his mates to exercise their own initiative to that extent.

Only the children seem to be left free to enjoy themselves in their own way, free from organization by the state or the factory. Up to a certain age one sees Russian children enjoying themselves happily in the snow on home-made skis and toboggans. But never the grown-up people. Only foreign diplomats and German scientists and technicians are to be seen disporting themselves on the ski slopes of Bolshovo or Tsaritsino.

The children seem happy, cheerful youngsters full of fun and mischief—the same as in any other country. They do not wait for the state to organize their recreation for them. But at a certain age all that is lost. During the whole of my time in Russia I cannot remember, except at a theatre or similar entertainment, ever hearing a grown Russian laugh or whistle or break into spontaneous and joyful song.

To a certain extent the lack of individual initiative in sport is due to the impossibility of obtaining any sporting gear, even of the simplest, unless one makes it oneself. There is a small lake at Khimky, a suburb of Moscow, where a little sailing is to be had in the summer. But it is not possible for individual Russians, even of the class of higher officials, to own their private boat, simply because there are no private yards who could build boats for private ownership. It is not possible even to own a canoe unless you build it yourself, and even then you would not keep it for long. Absolutely everything must be done through a club, and every club is an off-shoot of some factory, which again is an off-shoot of the government.

The general outlook toward recreation for grown-ups

is that an individual's time is not his own but the state's. He should only require just that amount of relaxation and recreation to restore his energy in order that he may plunge once more into the task of working for the state. It is up to the state, not the individual, to decide what kind of recreation is best for him, or rather how much and what kind can be granted to him without interfering with the general running of the state.

Lest there should be any misunderstanding on this matter, I ought perhaps to make it clear that nothing which has been written on the 'lighter side of Soviet life' applies to the great masses of the unprivileged working classes. All these arrangements for holidays in 'sanatoria' and so on, are for the privileged classes of Soviet society— i.e., for the official classes and for the skilled industrial workers. For the great masses—the unskilled labourers in towns and the huge peasant population in the country— there are no such arrangements or, if there are, they exist, like many other institutions in that propaganda-loving country, only on paper. For the vast bulk of the toilers of the Soviet Union there is no 'lighter side' to life at all, unless one can count the occasional big national holidays. Even these are really little more than a change of occupation.

A very important feature of these big national days is the 'spontaneous demonstration of loyalty and devotion to the régime' which takes the form of a vast civilian parade. I have placed this expression within inverted commas because that is what these parades are officially called. We foreigners who have had the opportunity of walking round the back streets while these parades are being organized are inclined to take the word 'spontaneous' with a grain of salt. The thousands of 'loyal' citizens who crowd past the rostrum on these occasions may be 'volunteers' of a sort, but they are the kind which the British Army calls 'sergeant-major's volunteers'. Even on a public holiday the Soviet citizen's time is not his own.

CHAPTER IX

COMMUNISM IN THEORY AND
IN PRACTICE

MOST readers who have made a serious attempt to understand this formidable movement, Communism, will probably have read at least a part of *Das Kapital* by Karl Marx. It is doubtful whether many will have read the entire book, for it is extremely indigestible reading, even for an enthusiast. I have met many Communists who professed to have made a deep study of their own ideology, but whose ignorance of large parts of *Das Kapital* quickly disclosed itself during a discussion. They need not be ashamed of this; there are many Christians who are woefully ignorant of the Bible. But at least it helps to excuse would-be students of Communism, who are not Communists, if they also have been forced to give up the attempt to wade through the 'Bible' of Communism.

It is perhaps unfortunate that the English language does not lend itself to an easily readable translation of the more fashionable expressions used in the jargon of Communist ideology. Such expressions, for example, as 'dialectical materialism' and 'determinism' do not really mean much more to the average English reader when translated into English. There is no doubt that German certainly, and Russian also to a very great extent, are both languages that lend themselves much more readily than English to the discussion of deep abstract philosophy. Some may think that this is so much the better for the English-speaking countries and peoples, but I am not at all sure of this. It is always a good thing to know the other man's point of view, if only to disagree heartily with it. It is specially important for the ordinary man in the street to know what Communism professes to be in theory. It is important for two reasons. Firstly because Communist propagandists are adepts at being 'everything to everybody', and adapting their sales-talk of the moment to suit the particular customer. Secondly because, if the man in the street knows what the founders of Communism believed and hoped, he will then be in a position to judge how their followers today have modified the original theory to their own ends, and he will also be able to see how the *practice* of Communism compares with the various brands of Communist *theory* which are hawked about the world to catch the simpleton of every nation.

In China 'fellow travellers' are told one thing; in Spain they are told something entirely different. In one land religion of all kinds is anathema to the Communist propagandists; in another land they patronize with a bland and benign smile either one particular religion or the practice of religious belief in general. It all depends upon the type of fish to be caught. Thus, for example, at the moment there is a movement in progress to try to show that the 'early Christians' had much in common with the ideals of Communism, and that, in consequence, it is not impossible for a man to be both a Christian and a Communist.

I recommend all who are not yet convinced of the utter irreconcilability of Christianity and Communism to read what the great leaders of Communism have to say on the subject of religion. It is vitally important, once and for all to demolish the stupid and dangerous notion that there is some kind of 'Christian Communism' which is not such a bad thing. There is no such thing and there can be no such thing.

The theory of Communism is based upon the belief that there is a material explanation for everything, and that economic materialism rules everything and decides everything. In their view the human race has been undergoing a series of social changes throughout the centuries, each evolution being brought about by changes in material and economic conditions. Thus they enumerate (a) the Early Communal state of society, when the tribe shared everything and there was no private property, then (b) the Slave state, which began when the stronger and more warlike tribes subjected weaker tribes to slavery and robbed them of their lands and primitive possessions. Out of this grew the Age of Feudalism, when warring tribes, and eventually nations, each put themselves under the command of a leader who, in return for organizing the protection of the community, demanded and got certain services. Eventually the breakdown of the Feudal System gave place for the growth of Capitalism, according to the Marxists. The time is soon coming, according to them, when Capitalism in its turn will decay and collapse, and its place will be taken by State Socialism, which in turn will eventually give way to what they hold to be the perfect state of humanity—i.e., Communism. The important point to note is that they believe each of these changes of the past to have been caused by *material and economic factors*. They believe that these factors are already at work now, undermining the toppling structure of Capitalism. Marx himself said that he 'did not advocate the overthrow of Capitalism; he merely foretold it'.

It is very important for normal people to realize this firm belief of the Communist fanatics in the *inevitability* of evolution toward Communism. It helps to explain, amongst other curiosities of the Communist mentality, the chameleon-like changes of dogma which have emanated from time to time from the Kremlin. A notable example of this apparent inconsistency was the adoption of the N.E.P. ('New Economic Policy') in Russia under Lenin. This amounted to a complete reversal of attitude toward private enterprise, and is said to have even surprised some of Lenin's most fervent admirers. But the explanation for it all is to be found in his writings and in those of Stalin. What these explanations amount to is a bland admission that 'opportunism' must be the key-note of Communist tactics. It may frequently be necessary, in fact, to adopt some move which may seem to be in direct contradiction to the teachings of Marx. This will not matter at all, say the exponents of such tactics, if the Party keeps its eyes all the time firmly on the distant object. The apparent *volte-face* is not only legitimate but highly to be commended if it eventually leads towards evolution in the right direction. Believing, as the fanatics do, that evolution towards Communism is inevitable, it becomes easy for them to trim their immediate policy of the moment to suit

153

whatever way the wind may be blowing. This helps to explain such phenomena as the Hitler-Stalin Pact of 1939 and the recent *rapprochement* of the Kremlin and the Orthodox Church.

The non-Communist world must, however, take heed of this characteristic of opportunism in the Communist mentality and so must take apparent changes of heart at their true and not their face value.

I mentioned earlier the extreme indigestibility of the literature of Communism and the difficulty of wading sufficiently deeply to get at the basic structure of Communist theory. It is therefore very fortunate when occasionally an eminent Communist expounds in simpler words some of the ideals for which his ideology stands in theory. Thus Mr Gallacher, in a letter to *The Times* (17th Nov., 1948), defined Communism as 'a theory of society based on the proposition that the land and the means of wealth production should be the common property of the people and the foundation on which social relations should be established'.

This is a useful definition to use as a 'yard-stick' to measure the extent to which practical Communism of today is attempting to live up to its own theory. Let us study particularly the question of ownership of *land*.

About the same time there was published in *The Times* an obviously well-informed article on the successes of Communism in China. One of the main reasons given for the hold which Communism is obtaining over the simple peasant population was the fact that they were encouraging the peasants to help themselves to the land and peg out their own claims to small-holdings. I have, of course, no first-hand knowledge of the truth of this, but it is exactly the same as is being done under Communist auspices and approval in the Soviet Zone of Germany. The same bait of becoming owners of the land was held out to the landless peasants of Russia itself at the time of the revolution. The same bait was apparently used in Poland and several other of the satellite states of Central and Eastern Europe.

But how can this agrarian policy, of encouraging the peasants to grab the land and carve it into small-holdings, reconcile itself with the theory of Communism as propounded by Mr Gallacher—the theory of *public* ownership of land? For it is obviously no step toward Communism to take the land away from one private owner and merely give it to another. The answer of course is that it does not reconcile itself, nor does it try to.

The break-up of bigger estates and the parcelling out of land to small-holders is merely an opportunist step in the Communist campaign. It has worked so well in so many countries that it has naturally become a favourite trick. There never is any real intention whatsoever of leaving these poor simpletons of peasants in possession of their land for ever, or even for very long. As soon as the trick has served its purpose, the next step in the game is instituted—i.e., 'collectivization' or the forming of 'state farms', where the peasants, nominally free and honoured shareholders in a collective enterprise, in reality quickly become what they were once before—landless serfs.

155

It is important, of course, for the success of these tactics that the dupes should not be given any inkling of the next step till the time is ripe to spring it upon them. While touring about the Soviet Zone of Germany, we frequently used to chat to German peasants during our midday halts for lunch. It was clear that the scheme had reached different stages in various parts. In Mecklenburg-Schwerin, for example, masses of immigrants from beyond the Oder-Neisse boundary line were being granted a plot of land and a cow and installed as small-holders by the occupying power. In Saxony a different method was being adopted.

Once while driving in that province with a senior Russian officer responsible for military government and particularly for the agricultural side of administration, I asked him whether the system of collective farming had been tried or was being tried in Germany.

'Certainly not,' he replied. 'Why on earth should it be?'

'But we understand from your papers that it has proved to be such a complete success in the Soviet Union. If this is so, and if your people believe in it, presumably S.E.D. (the Communist dominated 'Socialist Unity Party' of the Soviet Zone) must believe in it also. It would be quite natural that you should apply the benefits of your own agrarian experiences here.'

The unfortunate man was in rather a quandary because there were also travelling in our car two people who, between them, were almost certain to take his words amiss whatever he might say—i.e., his own Russian driver, who might have denounced him if he had said anything against collectivization, and a German minor official, who might have 'let the cat out of the bag' to the local peasantry if he had declared himself a strong believer in collectivization. He changed the subject very abruptly, but not cleverly enough to hide the fact that here, as in many other countries, the Communists were offering the peasants one thing but secretly planning to deceive and later to rob them.

For what, in effect, does this agrarian policy amount to in the Soviet Union, where Communism has had thirty years in which to show the world what it can achieve? Mr Gallacher has told us that Communism as a theory is 'based on the proposition that land should be the common property of the people'. It will be interesting to study to what extent the people of the U.S.S.R., the vast bulk of whom are still countrymen and peasants, do indeed enjoy practical ownership of their 'common property' the land.

Many books have described the historical process whereby the Kremlin enforced collective farming and eliminated peasant ownership of the land, starting with the 'kulaks', the richer and more enterprising peasant owners, and eventually extending their campaign against all the peasants. I cannot of course add anything to these accounts from my own personal experience, because the process was completed before my time in Russia, but I can at least describe agrarian conditions as they are today.

There are two types of farm management today—*kolhozi* or collective farms, and *sovhozi* or government-owned farms. In the former the peasants *theoretically* are shareholders in the undertaking whereas in the *sovhozi* they are merely paid labourers in the employment of the state. Theoretically in the former case, which is the more usual arrangement, the peasants own the farm collectively as a corporation, and theoretically again they are supposed to enjoy the benefits of any profits made by the *kolhoz*. Each *kolhoz* usually has a market of its own in a neighbouring town, where its produce, *after deduction of state dues*, is sold in open market for the benefit of the people and for the profit of the *kolhoz* workers.

The catch lies in those words, 'after deduction of state dues'. In actual practice, by the time the state has collected its dues, there is remarkably little left for sale in the open market! In effect the lot of *kolhoz* workers is not very different from that of the *sovhoz* workers. In both cases the workers receive a mere pittance, just sufficient to keep body and soul together, and the 'state' gets the rest.

'But who, or what, is this "state"?' the Communist will ask. 'Is it not "the people"?' The answer is that in the U.S.S.R. the 'state' is the Communist Party, and the Communist Party is only about one per cent of 'the people', if as much as that.

The Communist will say that it may be true that the Party is only a minute fraction of the population, but he will claim that these public-spirited men act as trustees for the people as a whole. He will claim that this small and select band runs the state and among other things runs the land also for the benefit of the great mass of the people. If this is true, how comes it that the Soviet peasantry are still, after thirty years of Soviet rule, the most poverty-stricken, dejected, and miserable of any peasant population that I have ever seen in forty or more other countries of the world? How comes it that in a country like the Soviet Union, one of the greatest wheat-growing countries of the world, the population of Moscow, the capital, still has to stand in queues all night long for a loaf of bread? How comes it that none of the agricultural products of the fertile Ukraine ever seems to find its way into the stomachs of the poor working classes, other than the privileged few?

It may be true that this hiatus between the fertile soil and the worker's stomach is due to governmental inefficiency, or to the graft and corruption of a few bureaucrats, rather than to inherent vice in the agrarian policy as a whole. There is little doubt that inefficiency and corruption in high places do exist, and have been responsible for much of the trouble. In the spring of 1948, Liubimov, who was responsible for questions of food and agriculture, was summarily dismissed from his appointment at a time when the food situation in Moscow was going from bad to worse. Whether he was really to blame or was being made a scapegoat for the failure of the policy as a whole is an open question. When I left Moscow at the end of May the situation still appeared to be just as bad and the bread queues just as enormous.

But a policy which puts the distribution of food into the hands of men like Liubimov cannot absolve itself from blame if frailties of human nature cause chaos to arise. If Communism cannot be made to work smoothly and for the good of the people in Russia, where it has been all-powerful for thirty years, and where draconian penalties

159

are available to ensure efficiency and probity among the bureaucrats, there is good reason to doubt whether it can be made to work anywhere else. Let us first see Communism putting its own house in order in Russia, by ensuring to the workers a decent share of the produce of that very rich and fertile land instead of the semi-starvation diet on which they have to exist at present.

As with agriculture and the food which it ought to produce for the people, so it is also with industry. If the means of wealth production' were indeed, instead of only in theory, the 'common property of the people', there should be no lack of the more essential consumer goods in the shops and homes of Moscow today. Instead, on the contrary, there is almost a complete lack of the barest necessities of tolerable existence. One of the most flourishing among the small trades of Russia today is that of repairs to part-worn property of all sorts. Second to *Nichevo* (it does not matter) the word *Remont* is about the hardest worked word in the Russian language today. *Remont* means roughly 'repair', but in the rather rough-and-ready sense of cobbling, or patching, or botching things up. There are *remont* shops in every little back street for patching up every sort and kind of every-day article of use—footwear, clothing, pots and pans, tools and implements of agriculture or industry. Judging by the standard of dress and footwear of the normal people in the streets of Moscow, these little shops must be working overtime to keep the clothing and boots of the people from falling to pieces. Never have I seen such a ragged, patched-up, down-at-heel crowd as the average cross-section of

160

passers-by in the streets of Moscow. In the immediate centre of the city the standard is a little better, because here one sees mainly the wives and families of petty officialdom. The denizens of the outer suburbs, as I have explained before, rarely have time or money to visit the civilized centre. It is impossible to watch the bedraggled, listless, under-nourished crowds of the outer suburbs, tramping wearily round the daily drudgery of their existence, wearing clothing only fit for a scarecrow, without asking oneself how it is that the process of making 'the means of wealth-production the common property of the people' seems to have done the people so very little practical good.

Bad as the conditions in the outer suburbs may be, they are excellent in comparison with conditions in the more remote villages. In the remote country districts, inhabited not by the privileged industrial proletariat but by patient hard-working peasantry, conditions are truly appalling. Apart from the fact that these peasants do not have barbed wire and M.V.D. watch-towers round their homes, there seems very little difference between them and the inmates of a concentration camp. For both there is the daily round of work from dawn to dusk on a totally inadequate diet—a life of squalor, monotony, and constant terror. In both cases when they become too old or too ill to serve the state they just have to starve and die. In one respect at least the 'free' workers may have a slight advantage. If lucky they may be kept alive in their old age by the charity of other members of their own families, or by the Christian charity of church-goers, if they happen to live near one of the few churches still functioning for religious worship.

The treatment of the old and infirm is a feature of the Soviet way of life which ought to be studied by all who stupidly see some fancied resemblance between Communism and early Christianity. The Communist outlook is severely practical. When a worker becomes of no further practical use to the state through old age or illness, he or she in Soviet estimation is really better dead. It is a pity to waste food on 'useless mouths'. No provision is made in the scheme of things for the further sustenance of such 'parasites' (unless the individual happens to be one who has earned a pittance by way of state pension for some specially valuable state employment). For the rest, the ordinary non-officials, they must fend for themselves.

Consequently, outside every functioning church there is always to be seen a huge crowd of aged and decrepit beggars, whose continued existence on this earth depends entirely on the charity of a congregation almost as destitute as themselves, the poor non-official peasant community. Outside the great monastery of the Novoe Dēvitchie on the outskirts of Moscow on one Sunday morning I counted two hundred and forty seven of these poor old creatures huddled round the main entrance. Never in any other country have I seen human beings in such a state of hopeless degradation. The filthiness of their clothing was indescribable. Unlike the beggars of other lands these poor old wretches made no attempt whatever to importune the passing crowd. It seemed as if they lacked the physical

162

strength to do so. They just stood, sat, or sometimes lay along the path to the church and round the porch with one skinny hand stretched out motionless. Some of them had their eyes closed, and looked as though they were already dead.

Desperately poor as the congregation themselves were, I noticed that hardly anybody went along the path without handing out a few small coins here and there among the withered palms. Perhaps some of the alms-givers reflected that in a few more years they themselves might be taking their places in the line.

A favourite reply of the average Communist apologist, when confronted with these social facts, is to say: 'Ah! But present conditions, bad as they are, show a wonderful improvement over the conditions of Tsarist days!' If this contention is at all true, how comes it that the people are not contented with the progress made? What need is there for that immense police system to hold the people down, if the people are indeed happy and contented? Where is the need to make a secret of social conditions in the villages? Where is the need to prevent foreigners from seeing those conditions for themselves, if indeed progress during these thirty years of Communist rule has been satisfactory? Where above all is the need for keeping the Soviet people in ignorance of the standards of living in non-Communist lands?

Not only in respect of material comforts but also in the building of the national character Communism in practice seems to have fallen far below the fine dreams of its early theorists. The theoretical ideal has always been the creation of a 'class-less society' in which there shall be no exploiters or exploited, and where everybody shall work freely and willingly for the public good as self-respecting citizens of an enlightened and happy community. Instead of producing social uplift of that kind, what Communism in practice is producing is a nation of bullies and petty tyrants and police-informers on the one hand and a vast subject population of brow-beaten, terrified, and brutalized 'yes-men' on the other. The way to get on in a Communist society, or rather the way to avoid penury and dire want, is to inform on one's fellow citizens, to lie, to lick the boots of the M.V.D., to stifle one's better nature whenever one's conscience revolts against injustice and lies.

Whether police-tyranny is an inseparable transitional phase on the road to the Communist millennium is for Communists themselves to explain. There is no disputing the fact that it is an inseparable and outstanding feature of Communism in practice, and that it is rapidly turning the Soviet people into a nation of poisoned and perverted character. Communism, as practised in all countries where it has seized governmental power, is certain to poison the moral fibre of the people over whom it exercises its power. That in itself seems to me to be sufficient condemnation of the whole movement, for, even if it proved itself able to give the 'workers' the material amelioration which it claims that it is going to produce (but has certainly not produced yet), even the most wonderful material improvements would be too highly bought

164

for the degradation of human character caused by the Communist police system.

I admit that this condemnation holds good of any police state, whether of the Right or of the Left. But there is still a great difference between the police-tyranny of Communism and those of Nazism, Fascism, Falangism, and the rest. These other tyrannies at least show no sign of shame at the state of social life which they are imposing on their citizens. It was possible, right up to the outbreak of war in 1939, to travel freely and on one's own all over Germany or Italy. It was permissible to stop at little wayside inns without let or hindrance from the police. It was quite easy to talk freely to non-official Germans or Italians. It was even possible to stay as a guest with a German or Italian family. It is the same in Falangist Spain today. One can get into direct touch with the ordinary people and discuss social and economic conditions with them without fear of being made a victim of faked 'incidents' concocted by the security police.

These three Right-Wing dictatorships at least appear to have been unashamed of the social progress going on within their respective countries. They seem to have had no need to establish an 'Iron Curtain' or to institute any other precautions to stop foreigners from seeing how their people live. *If Communism has nothing to hide, nothing of which to be ashamed, why the 'Iron Curtain'?* Its *raison d'être* can only be one of two things—either to conceal vast military preparations for an aggressive war or else to conceal social and economic conditions which the Communists are ashamed to show the rest of the world.

165

If the Communist Party of the U.S.S.R. is genuinely proud of its achievements during thirty years of power, a simple way of advertising to the world the blessings of their ideology, and simultaneously removing causes of international suspicion and 'war-mongering', would be to open up their country to *free and unescorted* tourism. Above all let them encourage visits from students of political economy and social welfare, and let these visitors bring with them their own independent interpreters, so that they can go freely about the country, talk freely to the people, and form their own conclusions on what they see and hear.

At present the average Communist or 'fellow-traveller' outside the 'Iron Curtain', when confronted with unpleasant facts regarding conditions in Communist lands, has a ready answer. He merely dismisses all such statements as being lies. But there is one fact at least that cannot be dismissed as a lie—the existence of the 'Iron Curtain'. Let the dupes of Communism all over the world ponder this fact quietly to themselves. What is the 'Iron Curtain' there for, if there is nothing to conceal?

Reading over my diary, I can see that my attempt to remain an entirely impartial observer of Communism did not survive the first four months of my stay in Moscow. The principal factors that roused my horror of the system were, first, the police tyranny and its ruinous effect on the Russian character, and secondly the structure of falsehood and pretence upon which the political system is based. In December, 1947, some elections took place in Moscow, and it seems to have been this final farce which convinced me of the rottenness of the system.

One can understand and respect a political system which does not believe in popular franchise, and says so boldly, even though one may disagree with it. But a system which keeps up a pretence of popular franchise while making the whole thing a meaningless mockery can only inspire contempt.

Some days before the elections numerous centres of political activity, known as *Agitpunkts*, were set up all over the city. This institution, the *Agitpunkt*, is a combination of a political lecture hall and a polling booth with a faint 'club' atmosphere included. Every artifice of propaganda is employed within their precincts. Nominally proceedings take the form of 'discussions', but in practice the discussion is distinctly one-sided. It consists mainly of a monologue by a selected Party member, followed by a few timid and innocuous questions. Sometimes the speaker deigns to explain to the people the object of some change in governmental policy and the great benefits to be expected therefrom, but more frequently his speech is a monotonous repetition of slogans and exhortations to turn out in strength at the forthcoming elections in order to 'demonstrate the solidarity of the people behind the Party and the Great Leader', etc., etc.

Accordingly, on the 21st December the people turned out in their thousands to register their votes. They had all been told by the *agitpunkt* lecturers that it was the duty of every good citizen to do so. In Russia that means that it will be regarded as a sign of a bad citizen to desist from going to the poll. Nobody cares to take this risk in a land where absentees would certainly be noticed, if not denounced by their next-door neighbours.

I spent the day wandering round the polling booths to watch the people performing this important and responsible civic duty. The whole thing was a farce and the people knew it. There was a list of candidates, every one of them Communists, already selected and approved by local branches of the Party (acting through local committees, factory committees, etc.). Even the very lists of candidates were farcical. There might, for example, be four candidates for a certain constituency, but if you read the list carefully you would find that perhaps three out of the four names would be well-known leaders of the Party such as Stalin, Beria, Molotov, etc. This adoption of the great ones as candidates for about ninety-nine per cent of constituencies is not merely a childish piece of sycophancy, but it has also a practical purpose. It ensures that the 'leaders' receive an 'overwhelming vote of confidence' from the electorate as a whole, and at the same time leaves number four on the list of names as the inevitable representative of the constituency.

There is no more enthusiasm over these elections than there would be over the registration of names for a national census. Nor was there a spark of public interest a few days later, when the 'glorious' results were announced with a yell of triumph by the press. Nobody showed surprise at the results. The populace did not even pretend to be interested.

How can one believe that an ideology which is really

168

sound would ever be forced to descend to such contempt-ible tricks as these so-called 'elections'? Not even the people, on whom this folly is perpetrated, are deceived by it. It merely has the effect of creating cynicism and bringing truth and honesty into contempt.

It is because Communism has to rely upon force and trickery to keep itself in power that it can never attain to its own millennium of the class-less and state-less com-munity. For unless a social system brings about a gradual raising of human nature, chaos and anarchy are bound to ensue as soon as the restraining influences of police-tyranny are loosened or removed. The Communist way of life, far from improving human nature, demoralizes and degrades it. Therefore it will never be able to dispense with police-tyranny. In fact this force is bound to become more essential to the holding together of Soviet society as time goes on. Decency and human dignity, as restraining forces to prevent wrong-doing, are vanishing gradually as generation after generation grows up in an atmosphere of lies and trickery in high places. Eventually the only restraining influence will be fear of the police. This moral corruption, far more than its economic inefficiency and administrative muddles, is the really hideous feature of Communism.

Turning to the purely material aspect of its thirty years of power, one must freely admit that important progress has been made in some respects. Education of the people has made immense strides. Illiteracy is rapidly disappear-ing. The authorities seem to be making strong efforts to raise the cultural level of the masses. I was surprised, for example, in Leningrad, to notice the genuine interest taken in fine old pictures of the 'Hermitage' collection by crowds of very poorly dressed people, who in most other countries would probably have been incapable of appreciating art. Museums generally are well maintained and intelligently stocked, though even here the bias of ideology makes its mark. The culture of the outside world is only allowed to filter through to the Soviet people in a very diluted form. The great writers of the world are approved in so far as their works do not offend against the Communist doctrine, but, if certain portions of those writers' works hint at reactionary ideas, those portions are ruthlessly cut out. Till lately music was regarded as being incapable of ideological 'deviationism', but now even music can be suspect. I have already mentioned the campaign against prominent Soviet composers on the fantastic charge of 'formalism'. But apart from such oddities, the authorities do seem to be making a praiseworthy effort to raise the cultural standard of their people.

In the realm of purely physical amenities much improvement has been achieved during the last thirty years. As I have shown in Chapter III, very much still remains to be done. The standard of living of the people as a whole is deplorable. But improvements and present shortcomings are both of them only comparatively unimportant standards by which to judge the success or otherwise of the Communist régime in Russia. Wholesale electrification, whereby there is scarcely a hovel within a hundred miles of Moscow that has not got electric light, is certainly an achievement, but it is probable that even Tsarism, had it survived, would have produced at least some electrification by now. It is obviously not fair to compare the material achievements of 1948 with those of 1917.

Outstanding among achievements of the Communist régime are great public works such as the Moscow-Volga Canal, the Saratov gas scheme (whereby natural gas from Saratov on the Volga is brought by pipe-line many hundred miles across country to Moscow) and the great network of electric power and light which covers the country. In the sphere of public amenities praise is due to the public transport services of Moscow, particularly the 'Metro' underground railway.

The general policy of the Kremlin, in the matter of material improvement, seems to be to aim at what they consider to be an adequate standard of living for the workers. The fact that this standard is terribly low by any non-Soviet standards may be due to a variety of causes. It is certainly not a good advertisement for Communism. It may not necessarily in itself be a fault attributable to that ideology. Indeed the terrible conditions of the Soviet people might be a cause for sympathy toward the Soviet government in its difficulties, were it not for the fact that the Kremlin, by its own secrecy and obvious desire to hide these conditions, implies a certain guilty knowledge that some at least of the trouble may fairly be attributed to their attempts to make Communism work.

To sort out the avoidable from the inevitable reasons for the deplorable economic conditions of the people would require the technical knowledge of an expert on political

171

economy, which I am not. I therefore can only describe those conditions as I saw them (see Chapter III) without attempting to assign how much of the blame is due to Communism and how much to natural causes.

This book may no doubt be read by Communists and by many who are strongly attracted toward Communistic ideas. The true 'hard-boiled' Communist will dismiss all that I write as a pack of lies, written by an incorrigible reactionary. The dabbler in Communist ideology may likewise try to suppress any doubts or misgivings. To such people I say:

'I do not expect you to believe me. I only invite you to ponder certain *indisputable* facts. The "Iron Curtain" is one of these facts. If the words of this book are not true, why does the "Iron Curtain" exist? The constant trickle of Soviet citizens out of the Soviet Union is another indisputable fact. Why do they want to get out, if my words are not true? There is no rush of would-be emigrants from the U.S.A. or British territory to the Soviet Union or to territories of Eastern Europe under Communist sway. Why is this? On the other hand many have endured terrible privations and dangers in attempts to go the other way. Shortly before I left Moscow two Spaniards, ardent Communists who had fought against Franco, were caught by the Soviet authorities trying to smuggle themselves out of the country in packing cases. There have been many authenticated instances of Esthonians and others braving the rigours of a long sea voyage crowded into some frail open boat, rather than stay any longer to enjoy the so-called "blessings" of Communism. Why do all these poor people undergo acute discomfort and danger? Why does nobody try to "escape" in the other direction?'

Finally, to those whose Communism is so 'hard-boiled' as to be proof against such thought I would say:

'Well. Go to the Soviet Union and see things for yourself. Go as a free, unconducted tourist. Go with someone who can talk Russian, and insist on wandering where you like and talking freely to the simple people. Or rather—*try to do all these things and see what happens*!"

CHAPTER X

SOVIET MENTALITY

DOES Russia want war? What are they really after? What makes understanding with the Kremlin so difficult?

These and many similar questions have been asked of me since I arrived back from Russia. This chapter will not be an effort to answer these questions (for only the Polit-Buro can do that) but to analyse the composite mentality which people seek to probe when they ask such questions about 'Russia'.

'Soviet mentality' is a product of Communist fanaticism superimposed upon the national characteristics of the Russians, the Belo-Russians, the Ukrainians, and many much smaller but none the less distinct nationalities. By far the preponderant element in the total population of the Soviet Union is Russian, so, although due allowance must be made for the possible influence of important men from the minor nationalities (e.g., both Stalin and Beria are Caucasians), it may be assumed that Soviet mentality in the main is a product of Communism and the Russian national character.

The Russian people by nature are neither bellicose nor hostile to foreigners—or at any rate no more so than the usual wariness of uncultured peasants for any stranger. This local 'insularity' is common to peasants all over the world and is quite a different thing to xenophobia or dislike of foreigners as such. It would be applied just as strongly to a man from Leningrad, if he settled in some small village on the lower Volga as it would be toward an out-and-out foreigner. There is no sense of hostility in this peasant feeling of 'insularity' when left to itself, but it lends itself readily enough to conversion by astute propaganda into temporary flashes of xenophobia.

If by 'Russia' is meant the ordinary non-official masses who comprise ninety-five per cent of the population, the answer to the first question would be an easy one. These simple people most definitely do not want war any more than do the ordinary simple people of any other country. But unfortunately in the Soviet Union, even less than in any other country, these ordinary non-official masses have little voice in the matter. This does not, however, mean that public opinion can be ignored altogether, even in a totalitarian country.

The Polit-Buro oligarchy knows full well that successful war cannot be waged without at least a measure of popular support. They know that this is particularly the case with Russia. There have been two great wars in modern times wherein Russian arms were triumphant—against Napoleon in 1812 and against Hitler in 1944-45. In both these cases the war seemed to the masses of the people a struggle to rid the fatherland of an invader. There have been on the other hand two wars which ended in disaster and defeat for Russia—the war of 1914-17 and the Russo-Japanese war. In neither of these cases was popular support stirred up. The masses of the people were indifferent to both these wars, if not actively opposed to them. This lesson cannot have failed to impress itself on the leaders of the Soviet

175

Union. It is easy enough to stir up the simple masses to patriotic fervour against an actual invader of the sacred soil of the fatherland, but not so easy to win enthusiasm for a war of foreign aggression outside Soviet territory.

This problem in itself would not present unsurmountable difficulties to the technicians of totalitarian propaganda. It would be comparatively simple to concoct stories of unprovoked aggression by the Western Powers, and to support these stories by faked photographs of atrocities and all the other tricks of the totalitarian propagandist bureaux. But it might be considerably more difficult to get the people to believe these tales. Soviet propaganda has been overdone to such an extent that even the most gullible among Soviet citizens are not influenced deeply by it.

This particularly applies to the constant stream of abuse against foreigners which pours forth from the Soviet press. In spite of unceasing anti-foreign propaganda there is little or no sign of xenophobia among the ordinary people. In fact the stream of propaganda seems to have rather the opposite effect. After the outburst of press attacks against me in the 'affair of the old sheepskin coat' I certainly found that the ordinary Russians with whom I had dealings were noticeably more friendly than before the attacks were made. Even Soviet officials frequently give the impression that they are being offensive in obedience to orders from above and very much against their own personal feelings. I feel that I may justifiably claim to have probed the depths of xenophobia more thoroughly than many resident foreigners. The affair of the village mob may seem to contradict my theory that xenophobia is not rampant. On the contrary I suggest that it tends to prove this. The village mob set upon me, not because I was a foreigner, but because they had been told that I was a dangerous and armed desperado. They would have done exactly the same to a Russian under similar circumstances. The fact that they took my side against the forester, when he was shown to be a liar, though by then they knew that I was a foreigner, seems to indicate that it was not a question of hostility to foreigners.

The intensity of governmental efforts to stir up anti-foreign feeling is an indication both of the importance attached to public support and at the same time their dissatisfaction at the present apathy of the people toward the alleged 'foreign menace'.

Soviet mentality, this blend of Communism with the national character, manifests five principal traits. These are:

(1) Suspicion. (2) Ignorance. (3) Obstinacy. (4) The 'Yes-man' Complex. (5) An inordinate self-conceit.

Suspicion—'healthy suspicion', as it is called by the authorities—is deliberately inculcated into the growing boys and girls during their 'Pioneer' training. It is still further cultivated by environment as they grow up amid an atmosphere of lying, spying, underhand dodging of the police, and blatantly false newspaper propaganda. The more official the milieu, the more intense becomes the suspicion with which each individual regards his colleagues and the whole world outside his circle. Everyone is suspected by everyone else and each knows that he is under constant suspicion.

Ignorance of the outer world is astounding and abysmal, even among those in very exalted positions. This is understandable when one realizes to what an extent even the most powerful men are hedged around by the ever-present human curtain of the M.V.D. to prevent them from mixing with people of other nations and exchanging views with them. On my return from Leningrad in a Soviet ship, the *Sestroretsk*, one of my fellow-passengers was Mr Manuilsky of the Ukraine, on his way to represent his country at U.N.O. All prominent men of other nationalities that I have met are only too glad to take advantage of the informality of a sea voyage and the absence of official work to get talking to their fellow-passengers in order to obtain perhaps a new and possibly interesting outlook on affairs. Not so this great man. Throughout the voyage he was constantly attended by two plain-clothes men, who scouted ahead of him whenever he wanted to come on deck for an airing, so as to make sure that there was sufficient unoccupied space for him to incur no risk of having to talk to other passengers. It must be difficult, under such conditions, to form a broad and independent view of current affairs.

Obstinacy is a natural offspring of suspicion and ignorance. It is also intensified by the quality which I have called, for lack of a better name, the 'Yes-man Complex'. By this is meant the fear of doing anything on one's own initiative or of making any personal decision, if it is feasible to refer the matter to higher authority for a ruling.

This weakness is an understandable one in view of the ferocious penalties bestowed on subordinates if anything goes wrong, even if the mistake is due to circumstances scarcely within the subordinate's control. This naturally has the effect of making subordinate officials 'play for safety' whenever they can. What appears to be obstinacy in a Russian official may often merely be cautious post-ponement of action till he has had time to find out his superior official's views and instructions. An amusing instance of this characteristic occurred when the world first heard with surprise the result of the 1948 presidential election in America. Some journalistic agency collected the views of leading men of various countries and pub-lished short comments on the result in the words of each prominent man who was interviewed. All those interviewed gave their own personal opinions of the matter except Mr Vyshinsky, who merely said: 'I must have time to think this out'. He probably meant that he must have time to cable to Moscow to find out what to say.

Another offspring of ignorance is inordinate self-conceit. When one is brought up in the belief that the whole of the non-Soviet world is degenerate, corrupt, effete, and worn-out, it is easy to fall into the error of supposing oneself to belong to a superior brand of civilization, which is destined to become the glorious leader of a new world order. To give Soviet officialdom its due, this feeling of superiority does not exalt the Russian nation over other nations in quite the same way as did the Nazi idea of *Herrenvolk*. Rather it exalts the Communist Party of the U.S.S.R. as being the pioneers

179

and founders of the coming new order, and regards them as being the destined leaders (and incidentally rulers) of the rest of humanity.

'The Russian is a charming person till he tucks in his shirt.' Kipling wrote this many years ago in the short story 'The Man Who Was'. The immense gulf in decency of behaviour which exists between officials and non-officials was evidently as great in his day as it is now. The ordinary non-official people are admirable folk—simple, kindly, fond of home and children and of all the decent simple things of life—very much like unspoiled country people all over the world. There is a rugged toughness in the Russian character. I do not only mean their physical toughness, which is astonishing; they also display a patience and uncomplaining fortitude which seems to enable them to endure without a murmur conditions which few other people would stick for long without violent protest. This trait in the national character must have been essential to a nation which for centuries has had to endure the rigours of life in such a land.

It is an extraordinary and unpleasant experience to see how the assumption of a little official authority at once turns a member of this otherwise pleasant race into a most difficult and sometimes obnoxious specimen of humanity. The average petty official is servile to his superiors, bullying and blustering to his inferiors or to anyone whom he considers to be in his power, stupid and obstinate in his dealings with equals of other nationalities, quarrelsome and quick to take offence where none is intended. The following anecdote will, I think, illustrate the best and the worst traits both in Soviet mentality and in the reasonable natural instincts of the simple soldiery or peasants.

This incident occurred in Norway during the process of liberation in 1945. It was my first encounter with Russians in the mass, and it taught me some useful lessons about them. The scene was a hospital camp in a remote place far north of the Arctic Circle.

In this part of Norway the Germans had employed many thousands of prisoners of war as forced labour for building their great motor road to the North Cape. The hospital camp was still full of sick and suffering Soviet soldiers, who were gradually being repatriated through Narvik and Sweden as soon as they were fit to stand the journey. It was a part of my job at that time to travel about Norway, ensuring that the Germans were carrying out their orders properly, and that all other arrangements were working as well as circumstances would permit. It should be remembered that at this time there was a serious shortage of motor fuel and transport, particularly in the far north.

It so happened that just as I passed through this locality, a lorry convoy of convalescent Soviet soldiers was due to leave the hospital on their way to Narvik railway station. I called at the hospital to see them off, and to make sure that all arrangements were satisfactory. I found embussing well in hand and everything apparently going very smoothly. I talked to the Norwegian 'Home Guard' who were organizing the move and supplying the lorries. They had made good and business-like plans on the basis of

181

twenty soldiers per lorry, which seemed adequate and reasonable. I also talked (with the aid of an interpreter then) to a Russian medical major, who expressed entire satisfaction. The soldiers were standing about in groups, waiting to board the lorries. They all looked cheerful and contented. All seemed well.

I wandered off into another part of the camp to supervise some matter connected with the German orders. Suddenly I heard a loud and ominous murmur arising among the Soviet soldiers. It was almost an uproar. I hurried back, guessing that something had gone wrong. Indeed it had.

Instead of cheerful and patient groups of men I now found an angry mob with expressions of surly discontent on their faces. A cluster of them surged round the Norwegian officer, who was obviously in difficulties. I marched up to the Russian doctor, who had now been joined by another Russian, a sly and shifty sort of officer, to whom I at once took a strong dislike. He was of a type that I was to get to know only too well later—a 'political' officer, not a real soldier at all—but at the time I did not understand these distinctions.

'What has happened?' I asked the doctor. 'Only a few moments ago you told me that everything was in order. What is all this row about?' The doctor, who I think was really quite a decent man, looked ashamed and said hastily:

'Yes. Yes. Excuse me just a minute. I am very busy. This officer will explain to you.' Off he went, leaving me with the fox-faced man.

'You surely cannot be surprised at the discontent of our soldiers,' he began unpleasantly. 'It is scandalous. These Norwegians have only sent enough lorries to carry our men if they crowd twenty men into each.'

'But your men and their doctor all knew that hours ago,' I pointed out. 'They seemed perfectly satisfied at first.'

'They are fools,' he spluttered. 'They do not know what is right. You cannot treat Soviet citizens like cattle.'

It was now quite obvious to me that this awkward customer was out to cause trouble for some obscure reason which I was at a loss to understand, not knowing at that time the workings of the Soviet mind. He was already on a fair way to success with his schemes, for things were rapidly getting out of hand. These men no longer had the restraining influence either of Red Army discipline or that of the German prison camp. Something had got to be done quickly.

'Call your men together,' I told him curtly. 'Round that lorry. I will talk to them.'

'You?' he sneered in derisive surprise. 'Can you speak Russian?'

'Not much,' I admitted, 'but enough. They are soldiers and so am I. Soldiers understand one another. Call them together.'

He did so. Meanwhile I grabbed the interpreter, and we both scrambled on to the lorry. The crowd gathered below. The little talk which I gave them was a strange mixture of German, English, Russian, and Norwegian, but they seemed to understand it. The interpreter stood behind me, and chipped in with an appropriate Russian word every now and then, which word I repeated loudly and with emphasis, as though it were entirely my own.

My subject was 'soldiers'. I told them that all the world had heard tales of the Red Army, of how tough they were. How could I believe such tales when I saw Red Army men whining like babies because they had to travel twenty in a lorry? All other soldiers that I had ever seen travelled twenty in a lorry. Americans did, and British, and Norwegians. Even the Germans. Was it really true that Red Army men were too soft to do so?

How much of this harangue actually 'got across' to the audience is doubtful, but at any rate I made them laugh. By the time that I had finished they were shouting, '*Nichevo! Fsia Khoroshaw! Vazmozhno!*' (Don't worry! All is well! We can do it!) and started scrambling into the lorries.

I have not told this little story to 'blow my own trumpet', but because it seems to epitomize most of the salient features of Russian character and Soviet mentality. You have the latent suspicion of foreigners, easily worked into a fury by agitation, the tendency to sudden outbreaks of violent tempers, and the vile malignity of the official schemer. You have also the simple mind of the peasant with his bucolic sense of humour, easily tickled by simple jokes, and quite open to reason if freed from sinister propaganda.

As in all countries, the composite national mentality is a mixture of good and evil. The good is mainly derived from the innate characteristics of the people themselves;

184

the bad comes almost entirely from the official outlook on life, born and bred from Communist indoctrination. It is a good thing for the world that the good elements do still exist, but it is a moot point how long they are likely to survive the constant indoctrination of rising generations with the evil virus of Communism.

M.A.

G

CHAPTER XI

WHAT IS BEHIND IT?

THE social structure of the Soviet Union is like a great pyramid. At the top are the fourteen men of the Polit-Buro, the real rulers of the country. Below them come the various strata of the Communist hierarchy, each stratum numerically larger than the one above and each taking its orders implicitly from the one above, and so acting strictly in accordance with the 'Party Line' as laid down by the Polit-Buro. Toward the bottom of the pyramid each stratum becomes numerically very large. These are the strata of petty officialdom, which has its ramifications in every form of human activity down to the individual house and its inmates.

The base of the pyramid is the vast mass of non-official people, and its submerged foundations are the unknown millions of political prisoners, working as slaves of the M.V.D.

The whole pyramid takes its orders from the Polit-Buro, the supreme executive body of the Communist Party of the U.S.S.R. But whence do these fourteen (or so, the exact number being variable) get their 'mandate', or the inspirations on which to shape their policy? For one thing is obvious from a study of the history of the Bolsheviks—that the 'Party Line' is not constant, but is subject to frequent and unpredictable alterations.

How else could it have happened that men like Trotsky, Zinoviev, and many others, who were once belauded as

186

heroes of the revolution, are now officially spat upon as traitors, reactionaries, and crooks? Obviously there must have been a change of ideological outlook. It is fairly certain that there has been not only one but several. What has happened in the past may well happen again in the future—a very important possibility to which I will return later. But what causes all these fluctuations of policy and outlook? How are they brought about?

These fourteen (or so) men, though collectively holding immense power, are of course both mortal and fallible. As they die off, one by one, they will presumably be replaced by the promotion of another 'stone' from the next stratum of the pyramid. In due time the whole fourteen will be changed, and an entirely new set of minds will be directing the policy of the Communist Party and the destinies of the Soviet Union. In the normal course of events this change spreads itself over a number of years, by gradual replacement, as when Zdanov died in the summer of 1948. This means that the new-comer or new-comers will usually be in the minority *vis-à-vis* the older established members. It would require a new-comer of exceptional force of character and personality to convert all the others to some new point of view, radically at variance with the existing 'Party Line', particularly if not approved by the formidable leader, Generalissimo Stalin.

Few know exactly how the Polit-Buro conducts its own deliberations—certainly very few foreigners. It is reputed that, during discussion of any new matter, each member can put his own opinion as forcibly as he likes, and that the views of all, from Marshal Stalin down to the most junior, are given equal weight. This may be so in theory, but in practice, knowing how human nature works, it is difficult to visualize the most junior member sticking too obstinately to his point of view, if opposed by the Leader and most of the others.

It is also reputed that, when once the 'Party Line' has been decided regarding any matter, all further discussion or opposition must cease at once. All, including those who might previously have opposed the new measure, must henceforth forget their original views and support the new policy whole-heartedly. Here again it seems to be asking a lot of human nature to expect a man to do this whole-heartedly, if he has previously held very strong views to the contrary. No doubt he must make a public show of loyalty to the new policy, on pain of being branded as a 'deviationist', but it is hard to believe that all can shed their previously held beliefs without any secret reservations within their own minds.

The 'agenda' upon which discussions, leading to changes of policy, are based presumably derive from 'public opinion' (if it can be so called) among the Party as a whole. The top men presumably have their 'feelers'—i.e. their methods of feeling the pulse of popular opinion and discussion in the lower strata of the Party. It is an accepted principle of the organization that 'criticism' (as they call it) is not only allowed but encouraged, *up to a point*. This criticism certainly takes place, and frequently assumes a form which appears rather unexpectedly subversive of discipline. Thus, for example, in the Red Army newspaper *Red Star* one frequently reads letters to the editor from private soldiers, criticizing the conduct of some tactical exercise, or complaining about the administration of a certain unit or the amenities of barracks. Knowing, as we do, that 'letters to the editor' in the Soviet press are not always the spontaneous and individual efforts which they seem to be, this queer phenomenon ought not to be taken too seriously as an indication of military discipline. But there is no doubt that 'criticism' within limits is allowed, and that it serves several useful purposes.

The most obvious one is that it affords a means by which the authorities may sense the general trend of thought. At the same time the fear of becoming a victim of this public criticism must act as a spur to keep all minor officials up to the mark. More subtle advantages are that it no doubt provides a handy method of getting rid of an unwanted official or of ruining his future career, the letters in this case of course being concocted by the head office, though purporting to come from the victim's subordinates. Finally this 'criticism' has considerable propaganda value among dupes of Communism abroad. 'See how broad-minded we are,' the propagandists can say. 'We do not try to hush things up. Far from resenting criticism, we welcome it.'

Besides this curious system of 'criticism' those at the top have other means of finding out what the lower ranks of the Party are thinking. It is up to any local Party committee, on any level of the 'pyramid', to put forward tentative suggestions and new ideas to the next higher stratum. Provided that these new ideas do not brand their authors as 'deviationists', no ill effects will fall upon the

189

authors. Whether the suggestions are acted upon or not, they at least get consideration and discussion on a higher level, and in this way new ideas can, and no doubt do, filter through to the top. Thus the Party as a whole can gradually and eventually influence the ideas of the men at the top, but on the other hand the men at the top, by their complete grip of the whole propaganda machinery (press, radio, *agitpunkt* lecturers, educational system, etc.) can direct and mould the trend of thought of the Party as a whole. The entire system conspires to make sudden changes of policy extremely unlikely, mainly because, neither at the top nor anywhere down the scale, would any individual be likely to have the courage to court certain death as a 'deviationist' by initiating any new idea which struck too loud a note of difference to existing dogma or policy. The outlook of the Kremlin is capable of change, but only rather gradually.

It need hardly be mentioned that only the two millions or so of Party members have any part at all in this shaping of future ideas and policy. The remaining two *hundred* millions or so of non-Communists naturally have no say in the matter whatever beyond the privilege and duty of voting occasionally for an already selected Communist to 'represent' them. It must not be thought, however, that the government is disinterested in the feelings of these in-articulate millions. The tremendous efforts expended on a constant flow of propaganda are proof that they are very keenly interested in making the masses think as far as possible in line with the Party.

There are several reasons for this. Firstly it is very much

easier to rule a people that is at any rate docile and resigned to the Communist way of thinking rather than one which may have ideas of its own. Secondly there is the very important aspect, already studied, of ensuring popular support, and if possible some patriotic fervour, before starting a large war. Thirdly the Communist Party of the future will be partly composed of the sons and daughters of these ordinary non-Communist folk, since accession to the Party is not yet entirely hereditary. To keep the future of Communism on the right lines it is therefore important to ensure that its ideas should be understood, and if possible held, even by the vast inarticulate masses.

Thus the policy of the Soviet Union is the policy of the Communist Party of the U.S.S.R. Its immediate interpretation and execution is in the hands of the Polit-Buro. It is therefore a matter of considerable importance to the world to know what the *real* aims of the Communist Party may be, as opposed to those which appear on the surface. It is not meet for a plain soldier like myself to attempt to answer such a vital question, for it requires a much deeper study of inner political history than has come my way. But perhaps as one who has mixed with all sorts of Russians, both official and unofficial, for two years, and who has studied the writings of Lenin, Stalin, Molotov, and others in the original, and who has read some at least of the propaganda stream in Soviet papers for two years, I may be able, not to attempt any final answer to this question, but at least to put forward certain personal ruminations which may assist others to find their own answer to the question 'What is behind it all? What are the real aims and objects of the people in power in Russia?'

It need not necessarily be taken for granted that the entire Communist Party of the U.S.S.R. consists of extreme fanatics, but it will be safer to assume that these have a predominating influence in the direction of its thoughts. There may be—indeed almost certainly are—many would-be imitators of Victor Kravchenko and Igor Gouzenko among these Party members. There must be many who have lost the original zest and enthusiasm of their Komsomol days, many who may even have seen through the beastliness of the whole system, and who have become disillusioned and disgusted. These may be subdivided again into two classes—namely those whose disgust will force them to break away at the earliest opportunity or take part in some movement for cleaning up Communism and its present methods, and those whose righteous indignation does not carry them into such dangerous waters. These latter will have decided to hide their disillusionment and disgust and carry on as members of the Party simply because that is materially the easier way of life.

This means that we can divide the Party into three kinds of members—the genuine fanatics, the honest (but at present secret) reformists, and the disillusioned but cynical careerists, opportunists, and place-seekers. We must assume that the first group has the prevailing influence, but a lot will depend upon what proportions the other two types fill both in the Polit-Buro and the Party.

It is very unlikely that any members of the Polit-Buro belong to the class of honest reformists, disgusted with the present state of affairs but sufficiently daring and high-principled to be plotting a change. It is too much to hope. The great majority of these fourteen or so must be assumed to be genuine fanatics, though there may be one or two unprincipled careerists among them.

What does each of these three classes want, and what might happen if one or other got complete power? The fanatics almost certainly believe that Russia has a sacred mission in history—to lead the whole world in the 'glorious' revolution which will (they firmly believe) usher in the Communist millennium. To achieve this end they are prepared to use any means. If they can achieve it by their present methods of 'fifth columns,' sabotages and propaganda throughout troubled parts of the world, so much the better in their opinion. But if it cannot be achieved without a world war, then they will have a world war, but not till the Soviet Union is in every way ready to take on the Western Powers in a fight to a finish. Till that moment arrives (and it is some way off yet) in my own purely personal opinion they would not even accept a world war if it were thrust upon them, but would climb down, shift their ground, accept any terms provided that these did not interfere with the continuance of the underground war of 'fifth columns', sabotage and propaganda.

I think that we must expect to see these fanatics, if strongly pressed, appear to turn over a new leaf and outwardly adopt a new policy of reconciliation, reasonableness and good relations with the outer world. Such an apparent change of heart will have to be watched extremely carefully by the Western Powers, especially if it happens rather suddenly after exercise of pressure by the West. 'The leopard cannot change his spots.' We must never forget that fanatical Communists regard themselves as being *already at war with the non-Communist world*. Fanatics of the Polit-Buro must therefore regard Russia, the champion and principal weapon of Communism, as being already at war with the Western Powers. Any trick is regarded by them as permissible tactics in such a war— e.g., adoption of an apparent attitude of reconciliation and international goodwill. The world must not forget the Hitler-Stalin Pact of 1939. Future pacts with the fanatical extremists would have just about as little practical value.

Turning next to the would-be 'reformists', there seems but little to be hoped from them at present. Any visions of underground movements taking effective shape are only delusions till the grip of the M.V.D. has been loosened by some other means. The most that these malcontents can do at present is to escape personally from the clutches of the machine, as Kravchenko and Gouzenko did, and by that act continue to keep the world alive to the magnitude of the evil.

Lastly there are the careerists, the unprincipled ones, who remain in the Communist Party for their own personal comfort and power. Their reaction to various crises in world affairs may be very different to those of the fanatics. It is probably fortunate for the saner portion of the world that such people exist in the Communist Party of the U.S.S.R. but it is hard to assess their practical value as a restraining factor without knowing who and how many they are. For obvious reasons every one of them at present spares no effort to conceal his cynical and careerist outlook by posing outwardly as a fanatic among fanatics. It is certain, however, that such opportunists exist, and that their influence will tend toward the avoidance of any rash or crazy attempt at domination of the world. These men are already in positions of enormous power and affluence. They rule, or have a share in ruling, one sixth of the world already. They will not wish to gamble all that they hold now on a crusade for Communism against the great powers of the Atlantic unless they are absolutely certain that the venture will not end in the same way as those of Napoleon, Kaiser Wilhelm, and Hitler. These men will use their influence toward building up power within the Soviet Union, 'developing and perfecting Communism in one state first', rather than trying to hasten the world revolution by a prematurely open challenge to the Western Powers.

This does not mean that these opportunists have any more affection for the West than the fanatics; merely that they have a greater regard for their own personal careers. They will not be averse to continuing the present 'cold war' against the West as long as it does not lead to the Soviet Union being forced into an open war before she is ready to win it. They will not lift a finger to prevent this Third World War if ever the moment comes when they, the cold-blooded opportunists, become certain that the U.S.S.R. can take on the Western Powers and win. That time is some way off yet, but it will come one day unless the

Western Powers do something about it first. Merely to suggest preventive action is to be labelled a 'war-monger' at once, but the correct term should be 'war-preventer'.

Now is the time to bring about a state of affairs where the 'fanatics' and the 'opportunists' within the Soviet Union will have to thrash the matter out between themselves. As long as both are satisfied that their present behaviour in the world is not going to lead them to a premature war, there is no bone of contention between them. If a situation arose where a choice had to be made between continuing their present 'concealed' aggression (and inviting a premature war) or dropping all their present aggression and living peaceably within their own boundaries, a bone of contention would be found. If such a situation happens while the U.S.S.R. is still unready for the Third World War, and while both 'fanatics' and 'opportunists' know that she is not ready, the latter would win the argument and there would be no war.

If, on the other hand, the crisis happens much later, at a time when Soviet war preparations are much nearer completion, even though not yet perhaps complete, it will be correspondingly easier for the fanatics to over-persuade the others that the gamble is justifiable. The risk of war under such conditions would be correspondingly greater.

If the crisis happens soon, and the alternative to war is made quite palatable to the 'opportunists', while definitely a set-back to the most cherished plans of the extreme 'fanatics', there is good reason to hope that these two factions may find it impossible to reach a peaceful compromise between themselves. In Communist politics such a situation results in a 'purge'. They have had them before, and would have one again if the necessary ingredient—an irreconcilable difference of opinion—arose.

A 'purge' in itself dislocates the machinery of the Party considerably, and in itself would be a factor temporarily, at least, setting back the schedule of Soviet preparation for war. So, even if the 'fanatics' won the day, and the more cautious 'opportunists' were to become victims of another 'purge', the victors in this domestic affray would still be faced with the alternative of accepting the challenge to a premature war (in an even worse state of readiness than before the 'purge') or else 'climbing down' and accepting the terms of the West.

What these terms should be is a matter for high statesmanship to decide. Presumably they would be sufficient to ensure that all further aggression and external menace emanating from the U.S.S.R. definitely ceased. Yet they must not be sufficiently severe to give the 'fanatics' justifiable propaganda for rousing the patriotism of their own people with cries of 'The Fatherland is in danger!' There are several things which could justifiably be demanded of the Kremlin, none of which by any stretch of imagination could be genuinely deemed an aggression against the rightful territories or economic independence of the U.S.S.R.

In spite of continual propagandist howls to the contrary, it is impossible to believe that any of the responsible statesmen of the U.S.S.R. genuinely think that the

Western Powers are plotting an aggressive war against them. Even allowing for the extraordinary ignorance of the outside world, to which I have alluded earlier, they know as well as we do that in reality there is no such risk, provided that they cease to be a menace to the rest of the world. The very most in the way of aggressive intention which they probably do genuinely ascribe to the West is an intention to prevent, at any cost, Communism from being forced on the rest of the world. To the extent that it is their own firm intention to force it upon the world, by trickery or arms, or a combination of both, they do in fact regard themselves as being *already at war with the West*. Their dislike of turning the 'cold war' into an 'open' full-scale war is our principal hope at present of making them mend their ways and behave as a normal member of the comity of nations. But the grounds for their dislike to take that radical step will decrease from month to month, as the gaps in their own preparedness are filled. The West will not avoid war by 'marking time'. They have every hope of avoiding it by taking a firm line, *as long as it is not left too late*.

This purely personal opinion of a private individual upon one of the greatest anxieties of the world today may not be worth a great deal. I have not been privileged to attend any secret meetings of the Polit-Buro, and have no clearer idea than any other outsider how they conduct their deliberations. These ideas have been based largely on as close a study of the leaders as one can get in a police-ridden and secretive country. It is possible, for instance, to form a fairly accurate opinion of prominent men by reading their political treatises and works, noting in particular what they have to say about one another. A fairly good idea of their characters can also be obtained by seeing how they go about among the people, or whether they do indeed go about among the people at all. The flat which I occupied lay within two hundred yards of Beria's city residence, and it was interesting and instructive to compare the precautions taken for his safety with those which Mr Winston Churchill, for example, would consider necessary. It is by little things like this that one can form reasonably accurate opinions of great men, and of their country's feelings toward them.

I have read what Trotsky had to write about Stalin and what Stalin still has to say about Trotsky. These writings are of course available for perusal, either in the original or in English, by any interested person, whether he has ever been to Russia or not. But to read these diatribes amid the atmosphere in which they originated, above all after mixing sufficiently with the ordinary Russian masses to understand something of the local mentality—these things do, I feel, enable one to 'read between the lines' a little more clearly than others can do, who may not have had the same chances of absorbing the 'local colour'. This is my only justification for airing my purely personal opinion on this terribly important matter.

When we leave the difficult study of the inner mentality of the rulers, and turn to the common people, here I know that I am on firmer ground. I am convinced that among the vast non-official masses there is absolutely *no* crusading zeal for the spread of Communism over the world, *no* xenophobia, *no* genuine belief that foreigners of any kind are plotting dark deeds against Russia, and *no* desire whatsoever for another war. Simple country peasants and ordinary industrial workers are not skilled actors or diplomatists. They cannot conceal their real feelings in these matters, specially if observation is based not on a five-minute conversation with one or two individuals but on a long series of talks with all sorts and conditions among the inarticulate non-political masses.

The rulers know this state of affairs as well as anyone else. They know that if they want the spirit of the people to be thrown whole-heartedly into another war, a great deal of preparatory propaganda work still remains to be done. This will require time, and extremely careful staging of the eventual *casus belli*, if there is one. There must be considerable disappointment in some official circles at the poor success of so much effort to instil a war-spirit among the people.

CHAPTER XII

CHRISTIANITY AND COMMUNISM

DURING the few months in England since my return from the U.S.S.R. one of the things which has worried me most has been to discover how many decent, honourable, and highly intellectual people there are in this country who appear to me to be indulging in some very dangerous muddled thinking. This muddled thinking consists in a belief that Communism as practised in Russia today is only one particular brand, a perverted and false brand, of something else which these thinkers appear to regard as 'true' Communism. This fallacy (for a fallacy it certainly is) seems to be particularly prevalent among certain eminent leaders of the Christian churches.

No less eminent an authority than the Archbishop of York announced (on Sunday, 7th November, 1948) that it is quite possible for a man or woman to be both a Christian and a Communist. He gave it as his opinion that there were two kinds of Communism—'Marxian' Communism, which he branded as non-Christian and evil, and 'Communism of the kind followed by the Early Christians'. He agreed that belief in the former was impossible for a Christian, but appeared to think that a Christian might legitimately call himself a 'Communist' without betraying the tenets of his faith as long as he only adhered to the second or 'early Christian' variety.

With the deepest respect I venture to point out that what the early Christians practised was not Communism at all, though it may have worn a certain superficial resemblance to some of the theoretical tenets of Communism. Or, to be more exact, certain of the theoretical tenets of Communism bear a superficial resemblance to the social arrangements of the early Christians. In this very resemblance lies a deadly danger.

Among the fungoid growths of our countryside there is a deadly poisonous species known as *Amanita Phalloides* or the 'Death Cap'. What makes it particularly dangerous to the unwary is the fact that it bears a superficial resemblance to the good and beneficial field mushroom. This analogy from nature describes fairly closely the relationship of Communism to Christianity.

Communism is a word invented to cover the teachings of Karl Marx and Engels. It is an expression that came into use only a hundred years ago, and is generally accepted throughout the world as being an ideology based on the teachings of Marx, and propounded in the *Communist Manifesto*. It is therefore asking for confusion of thought to try to tack this political label on to something which our predecessors in the Christian Faith practised among themselves *of their own free wills* nearly two thousand years ago. For, if a layman may presume to venture into theology, the 'sharing' of worldly goods, described in the Acts of the Apostles, was surely an entirely *voluntary* act of goodwill on the part of individuals, and as such it was utterly contrary to every conception of Communism. Ananias and Sapphira were punished, not because they were bad Communists, but because they were bare-faced liars. I hope that I have sufficiently shown

202

that under modern Communism they would more probably have been admired than punished for this action.

The communal 'sharing of goods' by the early Christians, which is so often misguidedly described as a 'good' form of Communism, was brought about by spiritual guidance acting upon certain individuals, who were free to share their goods or to abstain from doing so. It was a social arrangement, brought about by religious belief acting upon man's better nature. There was no compulsion at all about it. In all these respects it was diametrically opposite to Communism, which denies the existence of anything higher than the material plane, and both teaches and practises the notion that man can only be made to do good by force. Communism does not recognize any spiritual influence on man, nor does it agree that man has such a thing as a 'better nature'. It is therefore just as illogical and dangerous to describe those early Christian ideals as a 'good' form of Communism as to describe the edible mushroom as a 'good' form of Death Cap.

Even in those parts of its teaching which Communism has 'cribbed' from Christianity, there is a radical difference of outlook. Christianity believes in improving man's nature, slowly perhaps but fundamentally, till in the end 'public opinion' of a Christian community and the better nature of its members gradually abolish the evils of the world. It may be slow but it is permanent in its effects. Such evils, for example, as witch-hunting, badger-baiting, sweated labour of children, human slavery, prostitution, and commercialized vice, and many other evils have been stamped out in many countries and are being eradicated

203

from others by no other force than enlightened public opinion, inspired by Christian teaching.

Communism, on the other hand, believes in setting all the evils of the world right by force. It believes that man is an animal who cannot be spiritually improved and educated, since there is no such thing as spiritual values. To the Communist mind there can be no such person as a 'good' or 'kind' or a 'benevolent' capitalist, any more than we would think of a 'good' or 'kind' or 'benevolent' tiger. Nor would the Communist think of a capitalist as being particularly a 'wicked' capitalist. He is just a capitalist, in the same way that a tiger is a tiger, and as such he is automatically a menace to the 'working classes'. He cannot help it any more than the tiger can help it. He is only behaving in accordance with the material laws of nature. This is the first and greatest aspect of difference in the respective outlooks of Christianity and Communism.

The second great difference lies in the Communist conception of the individual man and his proper place in the general scheme of things. The Christian believes that every individual, no matter how obscure in the eyes of the world, is a person of particular and individual importance in the regard of an All-seeing and Almighty God. Communism not only denies the existence of any such supernatural being as God, but also denies that the individual human being is of any importance at all to anybody. Communism holds that 'Humanity' in the abstract, or in bulk, is the only thing that matters. In practice this 'Humanity' limits itself to one particular section of humanity only—namely one particular state (the U.S.S.R.)

204

CHRISTIANITY AND COMMUNISM

when thinking imperialistically or nationally, or one particular class (which they are pleased to call 'the Workers') when spouting for the benefit of their dupes in other lands.

I beg and implore all earnest and well-meaning Christians to dissociate themselves entirely from the dangerous idea that Communism in any form whatsoever is an ideology which can be reconciled with their religious Faith. For anyone to call himself a Communist, without believing in Karl Marx and his successors, is to misname himself gratuitously with the label of a dangerous and anti-Christian sect. Call yourselves anything else you like, if you believe in sharing this world's goods among those less fortunate; but do not call yourselves Communists unless you deny the existence of God, deny the existence of anything higher in man than the purely material, and consider the human individual to be a mere cog in a huge material machine. There is only one form of Communism—that of Karl Marx and his successors. Nothing else has any right to call itself Communism; it is dangerous and stupid to do so.

No doubt I shall be told that there are millions of people in Eastern Europe or in China who call themselves Communists even though they still remain believing and practising Christians. I have no doubt that this may be true, but it only adds strength to my warning. For these people have been deceived into thinking of something as Communism which does not clash with their Faith as Christians. Therefore what they have been taught is not true Communism at all, but something that will 'go down' with the local mentality and prejudices (as the Communists regard them) of that particular section of dupes and simpletons. The Kremlin has brought to a fine art the technique of 'trimming' their propaganda to suit local susceptibilities. They preach one thing to atheistic modernists, something else to Eastern Christians, and quite another line of propaganda to Moslems, Hindus, and Buddhists. They have got an attractive bait to catch everybody, and the more dupes they can catch and persuade to call themselves 'Communists' the better they are pleased, even if the form of 'Communism' which the dupes profess is not quite the pure brand. Of all types of mankind *real* Christians and Moslems are least likely to be duped by this blarney.

Every self-styled 'Communist', no matter what brand of so-called 'Communism' may have caught him, has become *ipso facto* a yes-man of Russia. I do not mean only those who have joined the Communist Party. It goes without saying that every Party member, no matter what his nationality, gets his orders from the Kremlin and has to obey them. But the vast mass of ideological dupes also, who have swallowed some attractive pill which they believe to be 'harmless Communism', have become by the act of swallowing it tools of the Kremlin and unwitting cannon-fodder in the underground war which the Kremlin has already begun to wage against the civilized world in China, Malaya, Burma, India, Kashmir, Palestine, Greece, and many other countries. Most of the so-called 'Communists' who are fighting under that label in these and other countries, would probably be horrified if only they knew the true tenets of the faith which they profess, and if only they realized its full implications on the lives of their own descendants. All these Communist fighters are ignorant 'mutts', stupid cat's paws pulling the chestnuts of world unrest out of the fires of civil war for the benefit of the Kremlin, the fourteen men of the Polit-Buro, who pull all the strings.

If Communist activity was restricted merely to those very few fanatics in the world who fully understand what Communism means and who have accepted it with their eyes open, the whole evil movement would die of inanition in a very short while. Even if activity was restricted only to party members (many of whom are cynical opportunists, not genuinely believing in Communism at all), even then the numbers of active supporters would be so minute in comparison with the total population of the world that the rest of the world would soon rid itself of this pest. But the strength of Communism as a disruptive force in the world lies in its devilish ability to enrol millions under its banner, by disguising that banner as something attractive to innocent but foolish men.

So it comes about that there may indeed be millions of true Christians in China, Eastern Europe, and even nearer home, who are fondling a viper in their bosoms under the mistaken impression that it is a kitten.

In this sense, and in this sense only, it is possible to be both a Christian and a Communist at the same time— i.e., if by the expression 'Communist' one means a 'dupe of the Communist Party.' It is very definitely impossible to become a *member* of that party without definitely abjuring Christianity and all other religions that are based on spiritual values or any notions of the dignity and high destiny of man as an individual. Without becoming a member of the Party, or at least aspiring to that 'honour', it is impossible to be any kind of a Communist except a mere cat's paw of the Party and of the Kremlin.

If any reader challenges my statement that it is impossible to be a real Communist (and all others are mere dupes) without abjuring spiritual religion, let him study the teachings of Marx, Lenin, and Stalin on this subject. Lest it be thought that Marx and Lenin may be out of date, and that modern Communism has altered its views about religion, let me quote the very words of Stalin which were reproduced, evidently with full official approval as being up-to-date doctrine, in the *Young Bolshevik* newspaper of late 1947. These were the words of Stalin:

'The Party cannot be neutral regarding religion, and it conducts anti-religious propaganda against all religions, because it stands for science, and religious practices are opposed to science, since any religion is contrary to science. ... There are cases in which some members of the Party occasionally hinder the development of anti-religious propaganda. If such members of the Party are expelled, this is very good, since there is no room in the ranks of the Party for such "comrades".'

This pronouncement was republished, with official approval, in late 1947, so it may be taken as a fair exposition of the present official attitude of the Communist

Party toward any tendency among its members to cling to Christianity or any other religious belief. This same paper also said at the same time:

'Religion cannot be a private affair of a member of the Communist Party, or of a Komsomol member. Komsomol organizations must allow their members no deviations from the theses of the Communist Party on questions of religion. The task of the Komsomol lies in active opposition to the influence of any other ideology on the young, including religious ideology.' Let it be remembered that this Komsomol organization is the gateway for the rising generation into the closely preserved ranks of the Communist Party, and that it is this party which calls the tune for all Communist (and pseudo-Communist) activity throughout the world.

It is useless for non-Russian Communists to pretend that they are independent of the Communist Party of the U.S.S.R. The whole world knows quite well that this is not the case. Those pseudo-Communists, therefore, who try to dabble in Communism without releasing their hold on the Christian religion are putting themselves under the control of an organization which is the sworn enemy of all religion.

Within the Soviet Union, in spite of the most violent and brutal persecutions carried out for many years, the great masses of the *non-official* population, particularly the peasants, are still fervent believers in the old Faith of their fathers. I took a great deal of time and care to investigate this matter, and was most profoundly impressed with

all that I saw and heard. I attended services, both Orthodox and Roman, on very many occasions, and am convinced that the most determined efforts of the Kremlin to
stamp out religious beliefs have proved a complete failure.
To see the unpretentious and sincere devotion of thousands
of miserably poor people, and to remember that only a
few years ago they were being fiercely harried for their
faith, and, as far as they knew, some change of Soviet
policy might re-start the persecutions at any moment—
these things were enough to fill me with profound admiration for the courage and 'guts' of these poor people, and
for the tenacity of their religious beliefs.

I had never previously had an opportunity of studying
the rites of the Orthodox Church, but it seemed to me that
the services were performed with reverence, solemnity,
and genuine faith. The churches, both Roman and
Orthodox, were always absolutely packed to overflowing
with worshippers, to a degree of overcrowding quite
inconceivable in England. In the Orthodox churches there
are no pews or chairs, merely a bare open space, but this
space was always so tightly crammed with people that it
was impossible for late comers to squeeze into the church
at all and almost impossible for the worshippers to kneel
down or even to cross themselves.

As a general rule congregations are drawn exclusively
from the non-official population—i.e., from the poorest
dregs of Soviet society. It is extremely rare to see, *at a
daylight service*, anybody well dressed or anybody who
could by any stretch of imagination be considered to be a
Soviet official or person of standing in the Party or the

State. But at night services, such as the all-night service of Easter, I saw many who must have been officials of importance. These were present not as mere spectators, but as active participants in the service, holding candles and generally behaving with reverence and true devotion. It seems as though, in addition to the poorest non-official classes, who have got little to lose but their lives by daring to profess Christianity, there are also many of the official classes who secretly retain their faith, but do not dare to make it too obvious to the Party.

I have often been asked why the Soviet Government is now tolerating religious worship, seeing that it is contrary to the teachings of Marx and Lenin and to the recent conduct of the Kremlin itself to show any such leniency. The answer can only be guesswork, for no outsider can know the inner working of the minds of the Polit-Buro. But the answer appears likely to be as follows. The government has probably resigned itself to the fact that, try as it may, it cannot suppress Christianity among the older people by persecution. Indeed it is probable that this persecution has had exactly the opposite effect. They probably hope that eventually religion will die out by itself, simply through the older and believing generations dying out and their places being taken by younger and atheist generations. Hence their anxiety to see that the Komsomol organization actively counters any tendency toward religion among the young. To what extent they will be justified in this hope remains to be seen. Personally I think that a great deal of Christian teaching is still

211

managing to filter through to the rising generations, in spite of vigorous Communist efforts to prevent it, and that a great deal of it is taking root. Officially no teaching of religion is permitted outside the churches.

Another motive for this degree of tolerance may be the fact that in the satellite countries of Europe the great masses of peasants are still fervently religious. Any open persecution of the churches in Russia might easily alienate what little enthusiasm can be generated among these satellite peoples for their Russian 'liberators'. Conversely a gesture of religious tolerance may deceive many millions of simple souls all over the world.

A third and more sinister reason may be some idea of making use of the Russian Orthodox Church as a rallying point for duped millions of Eastern Christians (and other Christians too, maybe) in a great 'reform' movement ostensibly aimed at the restoration of Christianity to its ancient 'humanistic socialism', but in reality aimed at destroying the spiritual influence and leadership of the Roman Church, which the Kremlin undoubtedly recognizes to be one of the staunchest bulwarks of the Western way of life against the world-wide spread of Communism. A great deal of subtle publicity has been given lately to this new version of an old idea of 'Moscow as the Third Rome', as it is called, the idea that the Soviet capital will become the spiritual successor to Rome itself and Byzantium.

It is an established fact that the Russian Orthodox Church supports the rulers of the Soviet Union. Toleration in exchange for the teaching of loyal obedience to the state is believed to be the basis of this arrangement. There

CHRISTIANITY AND COMMUNISM

is good reason to suppose that the lower ranks of clergy are not quite so happy about this as the rulers of the Church seem to be. It is to be hoped that the latter know what they are doing, and that they are not selling their own spiritual independence too cheaply. Even toleration from persecution may be too dearly bought if it links a religious movement to something which stands self-confessed as the enemy of religion in any form. When one watches the sincere devotion of the poverty-stricken worshippers in a Russian Orthodox church, it is hard to avoid the feeling that they might be wiser to remain poor, and an object of contempt or even persecution in the eyes of the state, than to risk their spiritual independence by running in such very dubious company. 'Who sups with the devil must use a long spoon.'

Sooner or later, unless the government mends its ways of dealing with its own nationals, the leaders of the Orthodox Church can hardly hope to avoid being confronted with a situation in which they will have to choose between swallowing their Christian principles or alternatively of breaking this uneasy 'concordat'.

There is a big clash coming eventually between believers in God on the one hand and the followers of materialistic Communism on the other. Men and women all over the world will one day have to make up their minds on which side of this fence they will be. It will be a sad thing for the Orthodox Church if they find themselves lining up on the side of the atheists through some sort of unholy alliance, which may seem plausible and astute at the moment, but which may prove to be a snare and a delusion. Any such diplomatic manœuvres will not, however, affect the religious staunchness of the non-official classes of the Soviet Union. To fanatics of the Communist Party their complete failure to eradicate religious beliefs from the people, particularly the peasants, must be a source of bitter disappointment and anxiety. In spite of twenty years or more of ferocious persecution and intense governmental campaigns of ridicule, often of a blasphemous and revolting kind, there are still many millions of practising Christians all over Russia, chiefly, it is true, in the country districts, but in the cities also.

This may seem to some readers contradictory to my previous statement that it is impossible to be both a Christian and a Communist. In reality there is no contradiction. These millions of poor non-official people, the working classes of Russia, are not Communists at all. They are merely the dupes and the pawns and the slaves of the Communist Party.

There are many who hold that the old pre-revolutionary Church of Russia was thoroughly corrupt, and that its elimination by the Bolsheviks would not have been at all a bad thing for the world. I can give no opinion on this because I have only hearsay evidence. But it seems that a Church which prevailed in Russia for so many centuries must have had a radical influence upon the character of the Russian people. Therefore, whatever there is to admire in the character of the Russian people (and there certainly is a great deal to admire), credit for these good characteristics must surely be given in part to the old Russian

Church. Her teaching undoubtedly produced in the Russian character a sort of mystic patriotism, on which was founded the tough fighting quality of the Russian soldier throughout the centuries. At the same time the old religion produced a sort of philosophical resignation, which has enabled the Russian people to endure patiently the rigours of a grim climate, the tyranny of governments, and lack of almost all amenities of decent human life. Comparing today the character of an average believing Russian with that of an average atheist Russian, there can be no doubt whatever that the finer qualities of the former are very largely lacking in the latter.

CHAPTER XIII

MISCELLANEOUS QUESTIONS

IN this final chapter I am going to try to answer some of the questions which have been put to me too late for inclusion in the main part of the book.

(1). *How comes it that you, according to your own report, were 'shadowed' everywhere by agents of the M.V.D. who spared no effort to prevent you from meeting Russians, whereas the Dean of Canterbury states in his book that he was allowed to travel freely everywhere and permitted to talk freely to all and sundry?* (This was asked by a Communist.)

I may already have given a sufficient answer in Chapter II, where I explained the very different treatment accorded to invited guests of the Soviet government (or one of its institutions) and resident foreigners. With due respect to the Dean I feel sure that his hosts realized that his political views were such that he could be trusted to see local conditions through 'rose-tinted spectacles'. I may have seen everything through blue or green ones, for no man can be entirely unbiased. But the point is that the Kremlin knew the Dean's outlook to be favourable before he was allowed into the country. With people of unknown views no chances are taken.

Not having been in Russia at the time of the Dean's last visit, I would be interested to know whether indeed he was given an absolutely free hand to go where he liked and meet whom he liked *without receiving any assistance whatsoever* from Intourist or VOKS or any similar organization, in selecting his itinerary or preparing interviews, or in any details of his travels. If he entirely dispensed with any assistance whatsoever from any of these agencies, he must be a most remarkable traveller. If he made use of any of these agencies, even to the extent of provision of a car and chauffeur, then he was in the tender care of the M.V.D. just as assuredly as any other invited visitor to the Soviet Union. Every one of these travel organizations works hand in glove with the M.V.D. These people are experts at foisting supposedly casual conversationalists upon the unwary foreign traveller in much the same way that a card-sharper can make his victim select, out of a full pack, just the very card that he intends his victim to 'select'. Though I was not in Moscow when the Dean last visited it, I saw several other parties of invited foreigners, and, like all other resident foreigners, I was left under no illusions as to the effectiveness of this 'shepherding'.

I am sure that even this further explanation will still not satisfy my Communist enquirer and those of his way of thinking. So once again I suggest to them all that they should try to do a sight-seeing tour in Russia themselves on exactly the same lines as one might tour about France, Belgium or Holland. I shall be interested to hear how far they get without 'guides' or officially provided interpreters!

(2). *What is the monetary system of the U.S.S.R.?*

The monetary system is based upon the paper rouble, whose value *vis-à-vis* the value of goods or other *real* wealth is entirely arbitrary, and susceptible to sudden alterations by governmental decree. Such an arbitrary change took place in December 1947, when all paper money then in circulation was deprived of its value as legal tender. Holders of this obsolete money were forced to hand it into banks in exchange for new paper money, but at a rate of only one rouble of new paper to every ten of old. To this general rate a sliding scale was applied. Bank deposits up to 3,000 roubles per head were exchanged rouble for rouble, and bigger bank balances at the general rate of one to ten. State loans were also exchanged at a slightly favourable rate. Full details will be found in the Appendix.

Briefly this bold and unscrupulous move showed the absolute power exercised by the state over monetary savings, and its readiness to juggle with the paper currency by surprise action. It is hard to say, even now, what effects these sudden alterations in the value of money may have had upon various sections of the community. The hardest hit class was probably the peasants, for, like peasants all over the world, they are inclined to distrust banks and to hoard their savings in their own homes. Added to this well-known tendency of peasantry there was also the practical difficulty of banking one's money regularly, if living in a remote country village. There seems to be little doubt that the peasants suffered severe financial losses, not only through having to change the bulk of their savings for one-tenth of their old value, but also as a consequence of the upheaval of the prices of market produce brought about by these monetary 'reforms', and by the abolition of rationing which synchronized with them.

A townsman (a non-official working man) told me with glee soon after these changes had been promulgated that in the Zagorsk district, about seventy miles north of Moscow, potato prices had fallen to a ludicrously low figure, and that the peasants had been left with great stocks of potatoes on their hands. A visit to this and other country districts corroborated his statement, but, in spite of this glut in the country, there appears to have been some hitch in the arrangements for transport to the capital or for retail distribution, for the town housewife did not seem to gain any benefit from the rural surplus.

Just as the peasants at one end of the scale must have suffered heavily from these changes, so at the other end it seems likely that officials 'in the know' as to the coming changes must have escaped without any loss at all, or they may in many cases have come out of the business well in profit. It would be astounding if it were not so. With so many sliding scales for regulating the rate of change from old paper money to new, anyone with an accurate fore-knowledge of the details of the scheme would have had no difficulty in ensuring that his own money was deposited in the right places.

Though every effort was made to prevent news of the forthcoming changes from leaking out prematurely, rumours of impending changes were rampant in Moscow for some days before the blow fell. A form of financial panic set in. There was a rush to buy goods and to get rid of money, and some extraordinary scenes took place. Any official with an accurate knowledge of what was really going to happen, as opposed to the many conflicting rumours, could have 'feathered his nest' very successfully. Apart from the dismissal of Liubimov and others in the following spring, an action which may have been due to a variety of causes, there was no outward sign of any reprehensible behaviour by officials over these transactions. This lack of outside evidence of such things proves nothing at all one way or the other. But, unless Soviet officials are all angels of financial integrity, it seems probable, human nature being what it is, that certain fortunes were appreciably augmented as a result of these jugglings with finance.

One other curious phenomenon of the monetary change was that, although all paper money lost its value and had to be replaced by new paper at one-tenth the value, money in the form of coins retained its old value. Consequently a ten-kopek piece is now worth ten times what it was worth before December 1947. One would require to own a vast number of coins in order to gain appreciably by this anomaly, but a gain could have been made by anyone who had been far-sighted enough to hoard coins rather than paper. As it was, probably the only gainers from this may have been the banks, who alone are likely to have been holding vast stocks of these coins. The banks, of course, are state-owned and governmentally run.

Apart from the formidable increase in queues for bread and other kinds of food, and the subsequent dismissal of Liubimov, this bold piece of financial and economic juggling seems to have been accomplished without a serious hitch. But it must have had the effect of shaking the faith of the people in the trustworthiness of their own government's promises and the permanence of value of the paper money upon which all economy rests. The old money carried printed upon it what was, after all, a governmental promise to pay the bearer one hundred roubles (or whatever each piece of paper was marked). Faith in the validity of such a promise cannot be worth very much now.

(3). *What organization exists for relief of poverty in the Soviet Union?*

One of the basic principles of Communist doctrine is to take 'from everyone according to his ability' and give 'to everyone according to his need'. The Soviet State certainly carries out the first part of this slogan very thoroughly, but it does not complete the latter part. If it did so, there could be no need for distressing sights such as the two hundred and forty-seven beggars that I counted on one Sunday morning outside the church of Novoe Dēvitchie. These poor wretches were only typical of similar crowds to be found outside any church. Their total number all over the Soviet Union must run into millions.

It certainly cannot be said of these derelicts that they receive from the state 'according to their need'. This seems to be one more instance of a discrepancy between Communist theory and practice. It would be safe to say that they receive nothing at all from the state, and are only kept alive through the charity of the Christian community. What then can be the system of poor relief, if any?

There appears to be a system, but it is based, not on the principle 'to each according to his need', but 'to each according to his usefulness to the state'. These poor old beggars are of no consequence to the state. They probably have no influential relations or friends. They probably never belonged to the Communist Party, or to any organization which might be offended if they were left to starve. They are all almost certainly Christians and not at all likely ever to have belonged to anything but the poorest and most inarticulate non-official stratum of society. So it does not matter to the state what becomes of them.

Even those who have served the state well do not receive much sympathy, consideration, or financial help, when they become useless members of society. This applies even if their disability has been directly caused by gallant service for the state. There is a pension scheme for disabled soldiers, but the amounts allotted are a mere pittance hopelessly inadequate for keeping the old soldier alive without supplementary assistance from others. It is a daily experience to see disabled soldiers, often horribly mutilated and imperfectly equipped with artificial limbs, going through the electric trains of the suburban districts, begging.

There is a serious lack of artificial limbs among these men. I never saw one of them with a properly articulated limb of the modern type. A certain number have the old-fashioned wooden stump, but vast numbers have not even that. One frequently sees men who have lost both legs, who get about the place with amazing speed and agility on a little wooden platform mounted on four small steel wheels. All these maimed soldiers have to beg.

The generosity of the poorest peasants is remarkable, and one cannot say that these disabled soldiers give the impression of being any more miserable or under-nourished than the rest of the population. But it strikes a jarring note to find these men, who must have deserved well of their country, so scantily provided for (if at all) by the state that they have to descend to begging for a living. The general impression is that of a Hogarth picture. One imagines conditions to have been rather the same in Western Europe after the Seven Years' War, when beggars and maimed soldiers abounded. It hardly seems to be in keeping with the dignity of a great state today—particularly one that preaches the doctrine 'to each according to his need.'

It is, however, in keeping with the callous but practical outlook of Soviet officialdom. Before rationing was abolished no ration cards at all were given to the aged and infirm. They were of no further use to the state, so they had to depend on the goodwill of other members of their household—or die.

What I have written regarding the inadequacy of pensions only applies to disability pensions awarded to simple soldiers and junior ranks, incapacitated in the service of their country. It does not apply to the pensions granted to superannuated higher officials. These are on a lavish scale, amounting in many cases to the grant of a house and continuance of the recipient's full salary for life.

(4). *Is Communism a permanency in the Soviet Union?*

Personally I believe that it is—in some form or other. All who dislike this mode of life in the present revolting form in which it manifests itself would like to feel that one day the countries now fast in the grip of Communism might succeed in throwing it off, and might return to a mode of life more in keeping with Western traditions of true democracy, individual liberty and decent self-respect for every man. I am afraid that all such hopes are based on an inadequate idea of the grip which the M.V.D. exercises over the whole country.

But, although Communism may remain in power as a permanency, there seems good reason to hope that in course of time, provided that its present viciousness is held in check, it may shed most of its present intolerable features and become a comparatively innocuous form of government for those who like it. There is historic parallel for this in the French Revolution. At one time it would have seemed ridiculous to any Englishman of normally royalist outlook to suggest that Great Britain could ever live on friendly terms with republican France. In those early days there was little difference between the loathing of the average man for republicanism and the loathing of the average man for Communism today. The republicanism of Danton, Marat, Carrier, and Robespierre fully justified that loathing and horror. But in process of time republicanism has become mild, respectable, and 'bourgeois'. Can Communism also become 'bourgeois'? It may sound to us now an absurd contradiction of terms, but so it would have sounded to our forefathers to suggest a 'bourgeois' republic, a pillar of decent international intercourse, such as France has been for very many honourable years.

This seems the only hope for the world, but I think that

it is a reasonable hope. Communism will not be stamped out by force of arms. That will only drive it underground, to become a far more insidious menace even than at present. But if the Soviet Union, as protagonist of militant Communism, can be compelled by firm action to keep its Communism to itself, and desist from all forms of aggression, the world may then see both forms of 'civilization' existing side by side for a period, each loathing one another as now, each trying to show that its own form of society can produce the greater happiness for mankind. If we Westerners are right in our ideas, as we know that we are, the final result will be inevitable. Though the way of life of the Soviet Union would no doubt continue to be called 'Communism', it would gradually be forced to abandon its more revolting features in order to bear comparison with the successful civilization of the West, till in the end some form of so-called 'Communism' will evolve, which will bear no resemblance at all to the bestiality of today.

It is not for us to try to cure them. They must work out their own cure for themselves. But, before that happens, the world has got to go through a most dangerous phase. The fanatics of this present bestiality have got to be shown that the civilized Western world does not intent to accept their poisonous ideology at any price. Till that lesson has been rubbed in so that no shadow of doubt can remain, the world will not free itself of its two nightmares of the present day—the insidious advance of Communism and the possibility of a Third World War. There is not much time to be lost.

MONETARY REFORM

Translation of extracts from the "Decree of the Council of Ministers of the U.S.S.R. and the Central Committee of the CPSU (b)" on Monday, 15th December, 1947, as published by *Pravda*.

Note: 'CPSU (b)' means 'Communist Party of the Soviet Union (Bolsheviks)' and the Central Committee, in effect, means the Polit-Buro.

AFTER a long preamble, explaining that the reforms had become necessary owing to (*a*) excessive printing of paper money by the Soviet State during the war to cope with the needs of war, and (*b*) extensive issues of counterfeit roubles by Germans and other invaders during the war, and (*c*) a consequent wave of speculation and hoarding of money by profiteers, the decree went on to say:

'For this reason the Council of Ministers of the U.S.S.R. and the Central Committee of the CPSU (b) have decided to carry through a monetary reform which provides for the issue of new full-valued money into circulation and the withdrawal from circulation of both counterfeit money and money without full value. This reform will be carried out on the following principles:

First. Exchange of cash currently in circulation and in hand for new money—10 roubles of old money for 1 rouble of new money.

Second. Money deposits in savings banks and in the

State Bank up to 3000 roubles—exchanged rouble for rouble.

Third. Conversion of all State Loans (except the 1947 loan) at the rate of 1 rouble of new bonds for every 3 roubles of old bonds.

Fourth. When the reform has been carried through the wages of workers and employees, and the incomes of peasants on *kolhozi* will be paid out in new money on the previous scale.'

The decree wound up with a propaganda peroration claiming that this method of 'monetary reform' inflicted far less hardship on the 'workers' than the post-war monetary adjustments of capitalist countries. It admitted that all classes of the people would be hit by the change of money, but claimed that (*a*) the speculators and hoarders would be hardest hit, (*b*) that the State was bearing the heaviest share of the burden of financial loss, and (*c*) that this would be the last sacrifice that the people would have to pay for the great War for Defence of the Fatherland.

Summary. These measures amounted to loss of nine-tenths of their savings by all who had failed to bank their money (e.g. the bulk of the peasants). Those whose money was banked escaped loss on 3000 roubles (about £100) but lost nine-tenths of the remainder. Those whose money was in State Loans got off lightest, losing only two-thirds of their money. Anyone forewarned as to details of this scheme could have escaped loss by judicious distribution of his money before the decree was published. The hardest hit victims were undoubtedly the peasantry.

INDEX